READER COMMENTS

Dear Herb,

Congratulations on being a Bronze Medal Winner of the 2013 Global Ebook Awards in the Teen Literature Non-Fiction category.

Congratulations!!
Dan Poynter

I knew Herb many years ago, and I can also understand why so many young ladies have adopted him as their grandpa. Herb is a few years older than I am. When he heard that I was going through cancer treatment, he was on his Grand Tour. That is his euphemism for being in Vietnam before most people knew Vietnam existed. Each week he wrote an uplifting and newsy letter. I never knew that war could be so much fun. He became like a big brother to me. With each letter, I knew that he was very concerned about my health and well-being. Later, I found out that when he knew he was going to be in harm's way, he would write letters ahead of time and leave them with a buddy to be mailed. He did not want me to miss my weekly letter. Reading his responses to his grand-daughters, I can see the same caring man that I saw many years ago. He is a little more mature, but the little boy pops up regularly. He now has someone to correct his spelling, but his caring nature shines through. I wonder if I am young enough to adopt him as my grandpa?

Laurie J., California

If we are lucky, the Lord blesses us with special friends to fill our lives. Some eight years ago, Herb and I renewed a college friendship when he introduced me to kayaking. I was instantly a fan. Since then I have seen people of all ages, but especially teenagers, become lovers of kayaking as well. Herb has a unique talent both for making people feel at ease, and for providing them with the confidence to attempt something new. Paddling alongside someone in nature's peaceful environment creates a time to talk and to share. Herb has used kayaking to listen and to gain the trust and confidence of his fellow paddlers. Many of his audience have become his "grandchildren," while others think of him as an "extra brother" that the Lord provided. Herb brings a wealth of life experiences to his advice for teenagers and guides them into discovering what the right choices for their own futures might be. Only a non-judgmental person and a great listener can win the confidences of teens. Herb fits the bill. I would definitely encourage anyone with teenagers or pre-teen children or grandchildren to sit down with them and read and discuss "Grandpa's" advice together.

Ann Bourlon, Seguin, Texas

Today I received a review copy of Grandpa, Help! - Answers to Questions a Young Lady Would Never Ask Her Parents. My husband had to wait for dinner since I could not put the book down and fix dinner.

Besides being excellent advice and presented in a great format, it is written in a humorous manner. Herb, I'm using his first name because I feel that I know him, has no problems admitting to his granddaughters that he was a JERK during his dating years. That makes his advice memorable. I wish I had had a copy when I was growing up.

Louisa F., Texas

I'm going to advise my sons that they should not consider marrying any young lady unless she has read all of the Grandpa, Help! series, and has decided to adopt the author as her grandpa. That way I can claim Grandpa as a relative. When I have granddaughters, these books will be mandatory reading for them.

Helen G., California

Our choices, big ones and small ones, create the quality of our lives! My husband and I have fun every day. We make it a point to find something to be grateful for every day! Today, we are grateful for Herb's wonderful book and all the memories of growing up that it brought back to us. We look forward to reading all of them, even though we are about four times the age of the intended audience.

Anonymous

All the grandpa stories are teaching something helpful in a fun way, so this book is good as well as being useful. There is some religious teaching, too, but it is not "in your face."

A lot of kids do not have relatives and people who love them without reservation. That makes life difficult because they do not have anyone they trust enough to go to for help. With so many hormones raging in their bodies, it is difficult for teenagers to make wise decisions in areas they know nothing about. So many kids are sexually active to some degree at increasingly younger ages. It is not teenagers only you should talk to. Many kids are now sexually active in elementary school, and I am not sure how that can be addressed, but it is a problem that must be addressed.

Winnie S., Texas

Herb Nordmeyer is the grandpa who goes where angels fear to tread! He will do anything to help young ladies who need his help. How do I know? Even though I am older than he is, I think he is blind, because he treats me like a cute 16-year-old, and he is always helping me.

Mary C., Alaska

GRANDPA, HELP!

Answers to questions a young lady would <u>never</u> ask her parents!

By:
Herb Nordmeyer and his granddaughters

Published By:
Nordmeyer, LLC
Castroville, Texas 78009

ISBN 978-0-9960100-0-9

Library of Congress PCN 2014909721

Cover design by: Ryan Ashcroft, Love Your Cover

Edited by: Katherine Puller

Formatted by: Herb Nordmeyer

Book Industry Study Group Headings

Family & Relationships / Parenting / Grandparenting

Juvenile Nonfiction / Social Issues / Adolescence

Juvenile Nonfiction / Social Issues / Dating & Sex

Disclaimer

We are not psychologists, counselors, or other professionals. We do not have professional licenses or degrees in these areas. We are two granddaughters asking our grandpa for advice and then listening to it. This advice has helped us, but that is no guarantee that it will help you.

Dedication

This book is dedicated to all of Herb's granddaughters and to all of those who after reading this book would like to be Herb's granddaughters.

This book is dedicated to all who would like to adopt Haleigh and Paisly as their cousins.

Acknowledgements

There are a number of people who helped get the project off the ground. First, there is my wife, Judy, who has given me permission to go kayaking with numerous people. If it had not been for the kayaking, Haleigh and Paisly would not have become my granddaughters. She has also taken my crude drafts and added punctuation, deleted repeated words, and corrected spelling. Then she lets me spend countless hours working on this series.

If it were not for Haleigh and Paisly constantly asking me questions, we would not have had anything to write about. You will become acquainted with them as you read this book.

Haleigh's and Paisly's parents have allowed their daughters to spend a great deal of time with me.

There is my daughter, Dana, who has furnished three of my over two dozen granddaughters. She understands that I am still a work in progress.

My editor and niece, Katherine Puller, has taken our nice prose and made it sing.

Then there are the people who have read the various drafts and made suggestions. There is no way I can list all of them, but here are a few.

I ruined Ann's saddle oxfords over 50 years ago. She has not let me forget it, but she has remained young, while I have grown old. She talked 14 bikini-clad young ladies, including one of her granddaughters, into giving me a hug. She wanted to see how uncomfortable she could make me. She gave me a cane because she knew my back hurt since my granddaughters had been wrapping me around their little fingers.

The Rev. Dr. Dan Mueller, my pastor for the last 15 or so years, has provided a great deal of encouragement and many suggestions.

There is the lady who was a year behind one of my younger sisters in school. We got very well acquainted as we traded weekly letters while she was going through cancer treatment and I was on my Grand Tour (euphemism for Vietnam). She has written numerous pages of suggestions and encouragement.

Winnie immigrated from Australia when she was about 20 years old. As she left Australia, a grandfatherly type man told her, "Men buy alcohol for ladies they have just met to open their legs." Her advice has been as blunt as that, and very focused on the pressures which men put on young ladies.

Mary always has an encouraging word and helpful suggestion, even after she moved to Alaska to start a new adventure when she was a senior citizen.

Craig is a deputy sheriff. He sees the seamier side of life. Not only does he understand what is happening, he is an excellent writer.

My sister, Mary, and for that matter, all of my siblings, have welcomed the young ladies who have adopted me as their grandpa, and have offered lots of advice without being nosey as to why I have so many granddaughters who are not my only child's children.

Christi, a retired Army nurse, arranged the Quinceañera which led to Paisly adopting me. She did the work, and I got the credit.

Come Join Our Community

This is the first in a series of books offering advice to young ladies. We published it as an ebook in 2013; and we are now publishing it as a print book as well. We are developing a website, *www.GrandpaHelp.com.*

We have set up a "GrandpaHelp" FaceBook page. Come and join us. When a new book is released, we will make an announcement on the FaceBook page, as well as on our website.

We also need questions to answer on our website and in future books, so send your questions to *Grandpa@GrandpaHelp.com.* Keep an eye on our website; post your questions on the forum when it is up and running.

Check in at our website and our FaceBook page on a regular basis. We will be giving away audio books, worksheets, and other helpful items on a regular basis.

Request for Review

 As you can see, I look very grandfatherly with my beautiful, full beard named Cassie. I'm planning on wearing Cassie until you post a review of this book on Amazon.com. To protect my face from clawing, all of my favorite granddaughters join me in asking you to please post your review as soon as possible. As you read this book, you will find that each of my granddaughters is my favorite granddaughter.

Table of Contents

Foreword

It's difficult to navigate life's challenging questions about dating and sexuality when you are a young person. Who am I kidding? It's difficult to navigate those questions at any age. But *Grandpa, Help* makes the process a little easier. I have been an advocate for youth development for over a decade now, and I have known Herb for more than half that time. *Grandpa, Help* is the book I wish I'd had when I walked alongside young people on a daily basis for my full-time job.

During the years I've worked in Youth and Family ministry, I've had my share of tough conversations with young people. Teenagers don't want platitudes or generic answers when they are tackling the problems in their lives. They demand truth. In this book, Herb deftly combines the two elements that I've learned are essential for talking to teenagers about sex, relationships, and life choices. Those elements are solid information and a sense of humor.

Herb's unique wit and his rich life experience shine through in each of his letters. His care and concern for his granddaughters is also very apparent.

Grandpa, Help!

Herb's advice is authoritative, compassionate, and relevant. Plus, he makes me laugh, which is always a bonus.

Herb is the type of guy who would give you the shirt off his back, so it is no surprise to me that he collaborated with two awesome young women to pursue this writing project. He has spent years listening to these young women, treating them as equals, and sharing in their joys and struggles. Mentorship doesn't just happen. It is a deep commitment that requires transparency and trust. It's worth noting that Herb and his granddaughters didn't just start out talking about tough subjects overnight. But once the ice was broken, the young women realized that their mentor had a wealth of knowledge to share about life and relationships.

It all started with an unexpectedly pregnant rabbit. This particular rabbit was entered into the county fair and won a blue ribbon. Very soon after receiving the award, the rabbit gave birth. The show rules stated that a pregnant rabbit could not be entered into the county fair, so the judges demanded that the blue ribbon be returned and that the rabbit and her young be removed immediately.

The next afternoon, Herb was in the kitchen with five or six teenage girls (he always calls them young ladies) discussing what had happened. Someone said, "I don't know how it could have happened; she got out of her cage only once, and that was only for five min-

Foreword

utes." Herb deadpanned, "It takes a boy less time than that to get a girl pregnant."

"**GRANDPA!**" Haleigh exclaimed. She was horrified. Herb's comment seemed so out of character that she could not find any other words to say.

Then Paisly's mother started talking. She took the conversation where Herb would never have dared to go. He was suddenly in a very explicit sex education class with a kitchen full of teenage girls. He knew he did not belong there, but there was no way to escape. The conversation was uncomfortable, but it was also vital. These young women needed to think about the consequences of their own choices. And suddenly, they had two adults who were listening to their problems and speaking to them honestly.

After that conversation, Paisly and Haleigh kept coming back to Herb for advice, especially when they were nervous about discussing something with their parents. Some time later, one of the young women suggested that they should collect their Grandpa's advice into an ebook. Along the way, that ebook has expanded into a series of books that is touching countless lives.

We live in an era when the generations tend to stay isolated from one another. Young people tend to connect with other young people, and older adults tend to connect with other older adults. This reality causes the younger generations to miss out on the wisdom and stories of those who have rich life experiences. It can have spiritual consequences as well. As a researcher-practitioner in the area of faith formation, I believe that having the generations together in dialogue is essential to passing on the Christian faith. When Herb shares life lessons with his granddaughters, he isn't just helping them navigate their teenage years. He is also having a deep and lasting impact on their spiritual lives. Grandpa, Help is proof that beautiful things emerge when the generations connect with one another.

Vanessa Seifert, PhD
DCE—Discipleship Catalyst
Calvary Lutheran Church, Lincoln, NE

Foreword

Introductions

Grandpa's

My name is Herb, and over the years I have had more than twenty young ladies call me Grandpa and adopt me as their grandpa. I've found that treating young ladies as equals and as if they are important (because they really are) forges a strong bond. These young ladies regularly consult me about situations they would never discuss with their parents.

Many young ladies are getting answers to vital questions from their friends, while others are learning about sex from their boyfriends. This can lead to mistakes that one can never recover from. My granddaughters and I have collected many of their questions and my answers into the *Grandpa, Help* series. The solutions we present are down-to-earth practical and generously laced with humor, so young ladies who start reading these books will keep reading. More importantly, they will remember the lessons.

I don't chide my granddaughters if they don't follow my advice, so they feel free to confide in me as they progress in life. By studying these books, young ladies will gain the understanding they need to become motivated adults who can become anything they set out to be.

For example, one of my sixteen-year-old granddaughters is currently sitting beside me writing the introduction to her own book. The advice we offer motivates, and it will help your young lady.

A Grandpa to those who need a Grandpa,
Herb Nordmeyer

Paisly's

Hello, Darlings, I'm Paisly.

I'm sixteen years old, and I love making Jim Carrey faces. It's good fun for a hermit, but I'm no hermit. I like baking, I am the class president at my school, and I love people.

You didn't want to know any of that, nor will you ever need it in your life. It's kind of pointless to read, isn't it? **This book** is worth reading; it's advice. I'm the girl who everyone comes to for advice. Partly because, no matter who you are, I will listen. Yet, I still have asked Grandpa countless questions. Before Grandpa and I met, I thought that by being an open-minded, compassionate listener, a sixteen-year-old could give the same advice as a 72-year-old. Oh, my lanta, was I wrong. (I'm going through an ancient

Introductions

phrase phase. It's groovy.) It didn't take me long to adopt this man as my grandfather.

Grandpa has more understanding than I ever thought possible for an old person. To be honest, I thought that older people could not relate to modern problems. Boy, was I wacked again. (Wacked: 1970s slang for wrong.) If you think you don't need advice from other people, then it is nice to meet you. You are just like I was two years ago.

I hate to admit that I sometimes need help. Grandpa needs help, James Bond needed his butt saved once in a while, and Edward needed Bella to stop him from showing his sparkly skin. Edward could have done that by himself; he could have just put his shirt back on. But he needed Bella to do that FOR him! See! Even the strongest of vampires needs someone to lean on and help him get dressed at times. Unless you're a pale, skinny vampire, you will probably need advice more than once in a lifetime. I don't really like taking advice from people, because I believe I can do it on my own.... But I can't.

Grandpa is the only adult I go to for advice. He not only gives advice, he explains why he is giving the advice he's chosen, and he does so in a humorous manner. He once recommended that I get a khaki-colored bikini. (Later in the book you will find out why.) Because I take Grandpa's advice, I've made many decisions I consider to be correct.

When I have asked my spanglers about problems, their advice has been all over the board. (Spanglers:

Grandpa, Help!

1980s slang for friends.) Every person I asked had a different opinion. It was confusing and frustrating, so I went to Grandpa and did what he said. Everything worked out. Everything would not have worked out if I had taken someone else's advice.

Another time, I waited to ask for advice. By the time I asked and was ready to change the situation, everything had blown up. It was a huge mess. Don't make the mistake I did. Do not wait. Why not read the information now and be ready to use it, instead of frantically searching for an answer when you are under pressure? BAD. Either way the advice is the same, but you're in a better position if you've thought about these issues in advance.

That's what this book is for. It was written to give you as much knowledge as possible about life. So pretty please with a cherry on top, read any chapter. They don't need to be read in consecutive order. For example, choose the chapter titled Why Am I Such a Disappointment to My Father? if it looks useful to you. Our questions are the same questions that you are going to have to answer in your own life, I pinky promise you.

Love, peace, and chicken grease,
Paisly

Introductions

Haleigh's Introduction

Hey, I'm Haleigh! I am sixteen years old, and I consider myself to be the only adult in my household. This definitely makes for some complicated three-in-the-morning questions regarding life and family matters (not to mention the fact that every boy my age is a jerk, has eight hands, and wants sex) that I honestly have no idea how to answer.

If you're anything like the rest of teenage America and you eat Nutella while you ponder why your parents took away your laptop again, this is the book for you. I'm not just saying that because I helped write it. I mean it.

For years, I considered advice to be overrated. Questions were kind of like pain—it made you stronger to have them. Then I got braces and broke my leg. I had to break down and take Tylenol and ask for advice. I got answers. Sometimes I got answers that I didn't want to hear.

In my experience, parents (or at least mine) can be very intimidating when it comes to questions, even questions as simple as, "May I spend the night with a friend tomorrow?" When you don't feel comfortable asking your parents, we hope that you can turn to this series of books for answers to serious questions about life, morals, ethics, careers, a family spat, or even a boy.

So, happy reading, and remember, these are real questions Paisly and I (and other granddaughters) have asked and the real answers that Grandpa has

Grandpa, Help!

given us. If two girls can mess up as badly as we do sometimes, have as many problems as we have, and still become successful authors with the help of Grandpa, I'm sure you will find that these books will help you as you travel the rocky road we have traveled. You'll be okay.

Haleigh

Preface

We are writing this series of books for several reasons. The initial reason was to help young family members. But, what is family? We decided to expand our definition of family to include all young ladies who might need the advice in these books or who need assurance that the questions they are asking are questions that other young ladies are wrestling with, too.

We plan on using a portion of the profits to help fund Paisly's and Haleigh's college educations. Haleigh plans to go to medical school and become a dermatologist.

During the years I worked for the government and in corporate America, I never placed any degree higher than my eighth-grade diploma on display in my office. Paisly has suggested that perhaps we should use some of our profits to buy a high school diploma for me to hang on the wall.

Recently I saw a note on Paisly's desk: "I mentor my grandfather on how to be a grandfather." You can see, I am still a work in progress.

Grandpa, Help!

Chapter 1 - Dating
Why Does My Boyfriend Grab My Boobies?

Grandpa,

My boyfriend put his hands in my blouse and grabbed my boobies. What can I do to stop this? Why is he doing it? I told him not to. He behaves for a few minutes, and then he does it again.

Your frustrated granddaughter,
Haleigh

Dear Haleigh,

Two years ago I told you that you could ask me anything and I would give you an honest answer. At the time I never envisioned that you would ask me about sex, but you have, and this is not the first time we have addressed the subject. I'm uncomfortable talking about the subject, and you probably are, too, but you have questions, so I will do my best to answer them. A promise is a promise.

Grandpa, Help!

As we have discussed before, boys are predators. Their DNA is set up so that they are driven to reproduce. In other words, they are trying to have little babies, but they don't want to take care of them. They figure that is your job. They just want to impregnate women, so there will be more little versions of themselves running around. It's not a conscious thought, but the way they are programmed. They are visual and easily aroused. They see something, and they want it NOW. As a result, they have a tendency to push the limits whenever they can.

Grandpa's Note*: One person who reviewed this manuscript stated that I was calling all boys sexual predators. There is a legal definition for sexual predator, but I am not using that term. Another definition of a predator is one showing a disposition to injure or exploit others for one's own gain. That definition fits the way many boys treat many young ladies. They are not thinking about the needs of the young lady, but just of their own needs. They need to grow up.*

Ladies, on the other hand, view sex differently. They are programmed to have relationships. They want to be held and assured that they are valued. This ensures that they will have help when they are raising a family.

Granted, there are some boys who are civilized and pay attention to what young ladies want. Notice, I refer to young ladies, and I refer to boys. This is done on purpose. As I said, some boys are civilized. They understand that young ladies have feelings, and they don't want to trample on those feelings. Unfortunately, a vast majority of boys really couldn't care less. If they can get part of what they want today, then they figure that they can push you to go a little further tomorrow.

I asked Paisly if she had found many boys who were civilized and paid attention to her preferences. She said she had found some, but that it was just about as hard to find one as it was to find Waldo. She assumed I knew about Finding Waldo. I'm honored she thought I was that up on modern culture. Then I asked her if she found civilized boys as interesting as predators. Her response addressed the heart of the problem, "Ah, the question every girl knows the answer to, but tries to ignore. Truth is, they get a lot less interesting when they aren't predators."

The fact that your boyfriend slips his hands under your blouse and goes exploring demonstrates that he finds you attractive. However, since he is going beyond the limits that you would prefer he abide by, he is actually dishonoring you as a person. Try explaining that to him so he grasps the concept while he has his hand on your breast.

You can eliminate the attacks coming up your blouse from below by always wearing a blouse that reaches about six inches below your waist. Get a three-inch-wide leather belt with sharp metal studs on it. Attach it around your waist as tightly as you can. You might also want to install a padlock on the buckle so your boyfriend cannot remove it. That should make it

Grandpa, Help!

more difficult for him to put his hands up your blouse and massage your front side. Are you grinning? The belt will cause him to change tactics. The hand will come down your blouse, or it may unbutton a few buttons for easier access. It will not stop him.

Before you go out with a young man, you need to make a decision about where the limit is. Only you can set that limit. If you're not planning on getting married very soon and a boy has his hands on your breasts, personally, I think you're going too far. What can you do to keep him from going too far? You want his attention, but you want his attention in the correct way. Tell him your limits before you accept the date. Don't apologize for having limits. If he respects you, he will respect your limits. If he doesn't respect you, he will not respect your limits.

If you set rules before going out with a boy, it will make your life easier. As your relationship develops, you can modify those rules. For the first date, you might state that holding hands is alright and so is a quick hug when he takes you home. If the first date went well, you may want to indicate that a quick good night kiss would not be out of line on the second date. By telling him that, you have paid him a compliment. He knows you like him enough to accept a kiss from him. He will not have to spend his time figuring out how he can steal a kiss when he takes you home. He can spend more time focusing on you. That is what you want.

My Boyfriend Grabbed My Boobies

Before you make out with a boy, in fact before you even accept a date with a boy you might make out with, the two of you need to have a conversation. I would propose you use these words, but you will need to turn them into teenage vernacular, "I know you want to make out, but we have to set some rules. You can touch me any place on the back that you want to touch me. You can touch me any place not covered by clothing. You can touch me any place on the head or on the face. That's okay, but don't go any further. If you do, you will be taking me home right then, and we aren't going out again, no matter how cute you are. No matter how much I like you, I don't want to take the risk of getting pregnant. You're going to tell me right now whether or not you are willing to abide by these rules." Refusing to commit to these rules means the boy wants to take advantage of you, so the only response you can safely make is to not date him. Remember, if you got into a wrestling match with him, he would probably win. You do not want that to happen.

While there is a segment of our culture that be-lieves in sex on the first date and having friends with benefits, there are many other enjoyable things besides going all the way. Talking for an hour or two is one. It will give the two of you a chance to get acquainted. Holding hands is one. Kissing is another. Going hiking is another. You could go to a movie, or do any of the hundreds of things you do with your friends. Going kayaking with a boy because he loves to kayak is another.

Grandpa, Help!

Grandpa's Note*: Haleigh is an experienced kayaker and often serves as my assistant when I lead wilderness kayaking tours or teach kayaking classes, so suggesting that Haleigh go kayaking with a young man to please him is said tongue-in-cheek.*

You have two hands. Even though it seems like he has eight hands, in reality, he has only two. If you are holding his hands, then he can't go exploring with them.

If you get tired of holding hands with him, then he may go ahead and try to do something else. He may start easy by moving up your arm. He will go a little further. When you don't object, he will go even further. It's kind of like world affairs. If the President does not send a clear message that says "You-all can't do that," then other countries may do things we would rather they didn't or act in a manner contrary to our best interests. Boys are no different than that. Strict boundaries have to be set up beforehand, if you don't want to be forced into doing things you don't want to do and are not ready to do. Failure to set boundaries and live by them is what causes young ladies to become pregnant before they get out of high school.

I know that several sixteen-year-old boys have sexually propositioned you. Apparently this is a very common situation, because these boys weren't brought up with the moral guidelines that were common before the sexual revolution of the 1960s. They say everybody does it; therefore, why don't we do it? If you say,

My Boyfriend Grabbed My Boobies

"Maybe" or "Maybe later," you have screamed from the rooftops, "Yes!" They know it's just a matter of time—a waiting game—until you give in.

Remember the blue ribbon that Suzie's rabbit won. The blue ribbon was lost because a buck rabbit in less than two minutes did what most boys will do in about the same amount of time, if they are given the opportunity. Pregnancy is simply the natural consequence. Suzie did not realize the doe was pregnant when she entered her in the county fair. After the blue ribbon was presented, the doe presented Suzie with nine baby rabbits. The show officials demanded that the blue ribbon be given back and that the doe and her young be removed from the fairground immediately. To make matters worse, Suzie did not get her entry fee back.

The excitement of having a boy pay attention to you, combined with wanting to remain popular with boys, makes setting limits very hard. The only way you can do it effectively is to set the limits when you are not faced with an immediate decision. You must also recognize that your future is more important than immediate pleasures.

Call me if you need help finding a belt,
Grandpa

This chapter will be the lead chapter in the book Grandpa Help!—Dating. Check Nordy-Books.com and GrandpaHelp.com for the publication date.

Grandpa, Help!

The next chapter, Why Shouldn't I Have Sex? I'm an Adult, falls into the category of sex. As you read it, remember that studies show that fourteen percent of condoms break. This exposes you to pregnancy and also to various sexually-transmitted diseases.

My Boyfriend Grabbed My Boobies

Chapter 2 - Sex
Why Shouldn't I Have Sex?
I'm an Adult

Dear Most Noble and Esteemed Grandpa,

Every time I'm alone with my boyfriend, he tries to get at least one of his hands inside my blouse. It gives me a thrill when he does it, because I'm an adrenaline junkie at heart. My mother tells me that I should not let him take liberties with my body. Why can't I? I can stop at any time I want, and if I don't want to stop, I learned all about birth control in health class. There is no way I would get pregnant before I am through college.

I love thrills,
especially the ones my boyfriend gives me,
Susan

Grandpa's Note*: I strongly edited the greeting to boost my ego. Boys do that, and all men are boys at heart. As you can see, I am having my granddaughter pat my ego.*

Grandpa, Help!

*Dear Thrill-Seeker Susan and
All of My Granddaughters,*

Paisly's sister, Suzie, entered some of her prize-winning, lop-eared rabbits in a county fair. A doe (that's a female rabbit) won a blue ribbon. The entire family was proud of the rabbit and of Suzie for raising her. The next day the doe kindled. (That is the word for when a doe gives birth to young. I wonder if the people at Amazon.com used to raise rabbits. Could that be how they came up with the name Kindle for their ebook system?) Since the rules for the fair stated that no pregnant rabbits could be entered, the doe was disqualified and lost her blue ribbon. Suzie was told to remove the rabbit immediately. The judges had handled the rabbit before awarding her the ribbon, but they had not noticed that she was pregnant.

We then discussed how the doe could have gotten in a family way, since she was kept in a pen by herself. Suzie said that the doe had been loose in the yard only once when there was a buck (a male rabbit) loose, and that they had only been in the yard together for two minutes. We concluded that he was one very quick buck.

I stated that boys are like that buck. It takes them only two minutes, and they can get a girl pregnant. Haleigh's mouth dropped open, and she looked at me as if she could not believe that I would say something like that. I continued that the boy has a wonderful time, like the buck, and then his involvement is over. The girl, like the doe, now has a family to take care of.

Why Shouldn't I Have Sex?

In the case of Suzie's doe, there were nine young, but in the case of a girl, one child is enough for her to lose her blue ribbon and change her life forever. That one little experience, whether totally voluntary or the result of coercion, completely changes the girl's life and will have an impact on the child she bears as well.

Sometimes the boy will stay around to help, but there just isn't much he can do. Most teenage boys cannot earn much over minimum wage. Even if he gets a really good job, the girl has still been saddled with the responsibility of raising a child. Even if he marries the girl, the divorce rate for those who marry in their early twenties is high. The divorce rate among those who marry in their teens is even higher. Will it really do the girl and her baby any good for the boy to marry her and then divorce her a year or two later? What will child care cost while the girl attends college, if college is even an option with a baby?

In the teen years, hormones start to flow in both young ladies and boys. The boys have a built-in urge to procreate. Boys usually do not realize that their urge is to procreate; they just want sex. Many young ladies want to have a relationship with a young man. This urge may be as strong in the young lady as the urge to procreate is in the young man.

The whole affair is complicated because these urges are new to the teenagers experiencing them. It is so easy to start with a kiss or two and a caress or two, and then suddenly find that his hand has slipped under your blouse. Then, OH, it feels so good when he

Grandpa, Help!

rubs his hand across your abdomen. If you let him get this far, he will see if he can go a little bit further. He is really not plotting how he can get into your pants yet. He is just experiencing wonderful feelings, so he reaches for a breast or slips his hand down the front of your panties. At this point if you reprimand him, he may respond with, "Doesn't this prove how much I love you?" No, it does not; it proves how much he loves the feelings that are generated by foreplay.

Yes, you have been participating in foreplay in preparation for having sex. Your body is getting prepared to receive his penetration. At some point your blouse comes off, and you lose your bra. Your pants are shed, but you feel safe, because you still have your panties on. At this stage it is very hard for either of you to back away. But if you want to stop and he wants to continue, about the only defense you have is screaming or appealing to his sense of reason. That is the same sense of reason he checked at the door about thirty minutes ago.

Most young men are stronger than most young ladies, and it may not be possible for the young lady to fight the young man off if he is determined. What happens next may be considered consensual sex, or it may be considered date rape. No matter what you call it, you just lost your blue ribbon. Rather than going to college for four years, graduating, and getting the job you desire, you will be taking care of your child. You may go to college, but graduating could take a number of years. Your mother may have to give up what she

Why Shouldn't I Have Sex?

had planned to do at this stage of her life to take care of your baby. Your father may get mad enough to get arrested for beating the young man up.

Can you understand why your mother might go ballistic when she finds you and a young man in your room sitting on the bed and innocently studying algebra? Have you ever considered that twenty-some years ago, she was having the same urges and being tempted in the same way? She probably responded in the same manner when your grandmother caught her sitting on her bed with her boyfriend, innocently studying algebra. How did she respond when the young man set his books aside, put his arms around her, kissed her, and then stretched out on the bed? Maybe your mother has had personal experience with what can happen.

Shall we go back and discuss what your great-grandmother said when she found your grandmother and her boyfriend innocently studying algebra while sitting on the bed?

In some cultures it is considered manly for a young man to have sex with as many young women as he can. In those same cultures, it is the family's duty to protect the women in the family. Don't ask me how they rationalize that, but they do. Years ago, I had a young man working for me who had spent five years in the Texas Prison System. He and a couple relatives beat an uncle to death with baseball bats for raping one of their cousins. When they approached the uncle, he claimed their cousin had invited him to have sex with

Grandpa, Help!

her. The young man and his relatives were protecting the women in their family; however, if the uncle's victim had not been a woman under their protection, these men might have been doing exactly what the uncle had done.

If you go out regularly with a young man, and he keeps seeing how far he can go, sooner or later he is going to manage to go further than you want him to go. How are you going to handle that? Can you back up and never go that far again? That is very difficult.

Then there are the young men who are up-front about their desires. They will tell you that since all of the other couples are having sex, that the two of you should have sex, too. Phrases like, "If you really loved me," often surface in those conversations. If he really loved you, he would be interested in your feelings and your best interests, not in satisfying his desires.

Another common line, whether said aloud or just implied, is, "I'll still respect you in the morning." That fits right in with the government inspector who says, "I'm here to help you."

Do you know what young men talk about when ladies are not around? Just take a wild guess. Do you want to be the topic of that conversation? Do you want your boyfriend, who claims he loves you, telling his friends that he got you stripped naked to the waist? This may be what he tells them if you let him get his hand inside your blouse. He needs to boost his ego, and how better to accomplish that than at his girlfriend's expense?

Why Shouldn't I Have Sex?

When he is trying to talk you into having sex, does he mention the other young ladies he has had sex with? If he does, you can be sure that your name will be at the top of the list when he uses this line on his next conquest.

Recently, one of my granddaughters told me that she knew of at least eight girls in her high school who were pregnant. How is that going to impact their lives? There are probably many more girls who got pregnant and had an abortion. In the case of those who chose abortion, will they ever wake up in the middle of the night and ask themselves whether abortion is the same thing as murder? They know that the Supreme Court determined that life does not begin at conception, but the Supreme Court made that determination based on political expediency, not on scientific fact. If a young lady wakes up with that question, will she determine that murder was justified in her case? Will it nag her for the rest of her life? This is a question that can only be answered after the fact, but if she is a caring person, the odds are that the question will nag her for many years.

I need to end this letter on an upbeat note. Yesterday I walked into the living room, and my wife, Judy, had the TV on. She was watching one of those afternoon shows where counselors try to solve family problems. The counselor showed a photo of a note that a mother had pinned to a bulletin board in her home. The note congratulated her son for growing up and indicated she knew that he would be entertaining his

Grandpa, Help!

girlfriend, Alexia, in his bedroom. She asked that he be responsible and use protection. The note had an arrow pointing toward a packaged condom. There was a map tack running through both the package and the note holding it to the bulletin board. The mother had inadvertently given her son a condom with several holes in it. I wonder, did he see the problem before he used it? Did Alexia even know that the condom was damaged? Would you like for that mother to help your boyfriend out? Seriously, would you prefer that your mother lecture you about the dangers of sex or that she actively encourage you to ruin your life? Would you prefer that your boyfriend's mother tell him to hold his passions in check or encourage him to take whatever liberties he wants to take with your body?

Birth control devices and pills work...most of the time, if taken according to the directions. The key words are "if taken according to the directions." That often does not happen. According to a study one of my granddaughters found, twenty percent of teenage girls who have sex regularly while on the pill become pregnant within six months.

Condoms work...some of the time. Studies show they fail fourteen percent of the time. Other studies show that fourteen to fifteen percent of women become pregnant within the first year of using condoms.

Withdrawing as ejaculation starts...seldom happens, no matter how many promises are made.

So far, the only birth control device I have ever heard of that works 100% of the time is an aspirin. As

Why Shouldn't I Have Sex?

long as you will hold it between your knees, you will not get pregnant.

If one of my granddaughters would write and ask me about the difference between love and lust, I would promise to not demean her feelings by referring to them as puppy love.

You didn't think I knew that much about sex, did you?

Love you all,
Grandpa

Grandpa's Note: *Sex has long been considered a taboo subject, but if you read the book of the Bible that used to be called the Song of Solomon and now is often called the Song of Songs, it appears that it should not be so taboo. It should, however, only occur within the confines of marriage. One evening Paisly and I read it together. Afterward, she said, "I wonder if my priest ever read this."*

When I fill out a form and it has the word "SEX" and a blank, I always write "YES."

This chapter will be the lead chapter in the book Grandpa Help!—Sex. Check NordyBooks.com and GrandpaHelp.com for the publication date.

The next chapter, Why Do I Disappoint My Father?, falls into the category of college, careers, and being successful. Since that is such a long tag line, we have shortened it to The Future. It

Grandpa, Help!

delves into why you may feel that your parent is disappointed in your performance. You will also learn why Grandpa is recommending that his favorite granddaughter obtain a khaki-colored bikini as part of the solution. By the way, each of Grandpa's granddaughters is his favorite. Somewhere in the series, you will find an explanation for this.

Why Shouldn't I Have Sex?

Chapter 3 - The Future
Why Do I Disappoint My Father?

Dear Grandpa,

Is it best to laugh at the little, stupid comments my father makes to me, or should I take them seriously? Like the other day when we were discussing my flight to Texas, he said, "I don't know if we will get her a one-way or a round-trip ticket." It drives me crazy and frustrates me. I know he loves me as much as I love him, but after so many little snide remarks, I can never tell if he's serious or not. He told me the other day, "Every joke has a little serious background to it."

Also, if I joke around with him, he just looks at me disappointedly. The "D" word! It's worse than any other word he could use towards me!

Gahhh... At school, I feel like I am a positive influence among my peers. I help anyone who is having a bad day or who just needs a friend. But at home I always feel like a disappointment. And writing this is bringing tears to my eyes. I strive to do the best I can,

Grandpa, Help!

but when it comes to my parents, I get frustrated and give up. Do I confront them? Do I try harder at home? Every time I turn around, I've done something wrong. Why am I such a disappointment to my father? What do I do, Grandpa?

Love,
A frustrated and confused granddaughter,
Paisly

Dear Frustrated and Confused Paisly,

When you come to Texas, I will maul you until you do not want to be mauled any more, and then we will talk about it.

Grandpa's Note*: For those of you who believe the word maul has a negative connotation, please read Chapter Six, I've Been Mauled by Love. For us, maul is a key word with a very positive connotation. It goes back to something my father told me when I was a teenager.*

I really like the idea of a one-way plane ticket to Texas. Then you can stay here, and we can see each other every day. I will not make the mistakes in dealing with you that your father makes. I will create a whole new series of mistakes, and you can write to your father, "I know Grandpa loves me as much as I love him, BUT...." Are you giggling yet?

Grandpa's Note*: The trip to Texas was for the purpose of attending a writing workshop.*

Why Do I Disappoint My Father?

Paisly came to Texas, and we attended. She was a tremendous success at the workshop, and we are proceeding with the publication of this series of books. She is also outlining a book that was suggested at the workshop - Grandpa Helps Grandparents. A book to help grandparents bond with their grandchildren.

Let's break the problem into two component parts. There are the snide remarks, and there are the comments expressing disappointment in your performance. We are making this distinction because it is easier to address the issues separately; however, as a practical matter, the two overlap considerably.

If a joke does not contain a kernel of truth, it will usually fall flat. That having been said, the kernel of truth might be the size of an acorn when compared to the statement, which is the size of a mighty oak. Are you now going to make a snide remark about my use of clichés?

A man will commonly make jokes at his wife's expense. For example, the bellman at a hotel says to the husband, "May I carry your bag?" The husband responds, "No, she can walk." It is often ingrained in men to make comments like this or to use other put-downs when referring to their wives. Each time a comment like this is made, it hurts the wife, but she quietly accepts it. Usually it takes an explosion before the husband recognizes the hurt he is causing.

I told a few jokes like this in my day, but when I was leading a marriage class, I learned how much

Grandpa, Help!

these comments hurt wives. So I quit making them. Here is another interesting detail about that class. While my friend Alice denies this, I can remember overhearing her say that I needed the class and the only way she could get me to attend was to have me lead it. When she pushed me to lead the class, finally I agreed.

Grandpa's Note*: Alice changed my behavior without directly challenging me. File that tidbit of information away, and use it in the future.*

Blonde jokes serve the same purpose, especially if the wife is a blonde. I convert blonde jokes to Texas Aggie jokes, because everyone knows that Texas Aggies have thick skins and nothing can hurt them. How's that for rationalization?

Seriously, I think that men practice jokes on their daughters to see what they can get away with before they try them on their wives.

My father used to tell me that to raise a son, it was necessary to pat the son on the back low enough and hard enough. This bothered me. I was about to say that my father never made snide remarks, but looking back, that comment does fall into that category.

Love,
Grandpa

Why Do I Disappoint My Father?

But Grandpa,

You are not answering the question I asked about why my father is always being disappointed in my performance. If I get an A in school, that is not good enough. If I fix his website, that is not good enough. If we are at a convention and I make a contact that results in a sale, that is not good enough. I should have made the sale. Nothing I do meets his standards. I can take the snide remarks. After all, the one-way ticket to Texas would not be so bad because I would be living with you, but he just is never satisfied, no matter what I do.

Love you,
Paisly

Dearest Paisly,

My father found that talking to me had more of an impact on me than paddling. In fact, he only paddled me once, and I must say that I deserved it. Usually he would just talk to me when I had done something he disagreed with. He was disappointed in my decision, or I should have thought the matter through better. He was disappointed in me. It would have been so much easier on me if he had beaten me. I know how much a father expressing disappointment can hurt.

My father always expected more of me than he expected of my siblings. When I was eleven years old and

Grandpa, Help!

my father started studying chemistry under my mother, I was expected to participate as an adult. I was not given any slack because of my age. My siblings, older and younger, got to go out and play. In fact, they were told to go out and play so that we could study.

Those chemistry classes, over a four-year period, led to my father becoming the Head of Research and Development for Pozzolana, Inc., and Rio Clay Products. At fourteen, I was working for my father. By the time I was seventeen, I was Assistant to the Head of Research and Development.

When I worked for my father, he expected much more from me than he expected from anyone else working for him. To make matters worse, he expected more of me than I expected of myself. One of the projects we worked on was developing a glazing plant for brick. I was put in charge of this project. After we burned the first kiln-load of brick, we found that there were black spots on much of the brick. He was disappointed that I could not produce a load of usable brick. There were also sharp glassy edges on the brick that would cut workers' hands. After we produced the next kiln-load, we unloaded it one brick at a time, writing down where each brick came from on the kiln car, as well as the condition of the brick's face. Since there were 3,000 brick in that batch, it took a while.

In analyzing the data, I found that if the faces of two brick were too close together, a black spot would develop. The solution was simple: leave more space

Why Do I Disappoint My Father?

between the glazed faces. Later I determined that this was a case of oxygen deprivation within the glaze.

There were other black spots, especially on the glazed surfaces that directly faced the inner walls of the kiln. These black spots were not associated with having the brick's faces too close together. It took several kiln firings to eliminate this problem. After the problem was eliminated, I concluded that the cause of those spots was the high-temperature mortar that had been used to bond the insulating brick lining the kiln together. Since that time I have determined that the problem was actually a sulfur compound in the mortar. The sulfur just had to be burned out. Whenever a repair had to be made in the kiln, we would dry-fire the kiln at a higher temperature than we fired the kiln when it contained glazed brick. That took care of the sulfur.

We found that the glassy knives attached to the brick were located near the outside of the kiln and close to the burners. My conclusion was that they were caused when the glaze was too hot or when it was maintained at the correct temperature for a few minutes too long. To solve this problem, I redesigned the firing schedule so that the entire kiln-load of brick would come up to temperature at very close to the same time.

I was very proud of my accomplishments in solving these problems, but my father never said that he was proud of me. He did point out that an architect had complained that when laying the brick up in a

Grandpa, Help!

wall, one could see a pattern in each seven brick. The first would be the lightest in color, and then each of the following bricks would become progressively darker. After seven bricks, the pattern would repeat. My father said that he was disappointed that I couldn't do a better job. After that, I studied the unloading process and the boxing process. The glazed brick were boxed in trays that held seven brick each. The man who did much of the unloading, would actually grade the brick based on color, and place the slightly-lighter-colored brick on the left and the slightly-darker brick on the right. Retraining him was one of the things that I was really proud of, but my father never commented that he was proud of what I had accomplished.

I would take the criticism, and finally when I had enough, I would raise my voice. At that point we both had enough sense to walk away.

I just could not wait to get away, get a real education, and get a real job. Eventually, I did. But then after a few years, I got back to using what my parents had taught me. My father and I became best friends. There are people, including your father, who maintain that I am the world's leading expert in pozzolanic chemistry and in stucco. So even though my father was always disappointed in me, he must have done his job well.

My first book, Stucco Handbook for Builders, went way beyond the things that my father had taught me. When it was published, he never said he was proud of my accomplishment; he said, "Who taught you all that?" I tried to explain that I had been learning while

Why Do I Disappoint My Father?

doing and learning while making blunders, but I don't think it got through to him.

When one of my sisters read the first draft of this chapter, she said that our father was much harder on me than the other children and that he refused to accept any failure on my part. He was a loving and nurturing father to her. She was the baby of the family, so maybe that explains why he treated her differently. I would have liked some of that, but if he had given it to me, I might not be the person I am today.

Now sit down, because I'm going to scare you worse than you have ever been scared before: your father is raising you to be just like me. When we went to the caves on the Rio Bravo Del Norte, you told me that your father had said that you would probably never see me wearing anything except khakis. I think it is time for you to start investing in khakis, so you can be just like your loving grandfather. Don't go out and buy the expensive designer khakis; buy the work clothes that the Dickies company makes.

You like to wear a bikini. What would you look like in a khaki-colored bikini? Are you giggling again? When you become frustrated while dealing with your father, take a deep breath and picture yourself in a khaki-colored bikini with an Audrey Hepburn smile on your face. Life really is good.

In conclusion, sit down and talk to your father about the snide remarks, but don't expect him to change his expression of disappointment. He has very high expectations of you, and you're not likely to

Grandpa, Help!

change them. What I would like you to do over the next few weeks is to think seriously about where you would like to be in five years and in ten years. After that, we will work on developing the goals that will help you get there. Then we can start selling your father on the idea that he should accept and adopt the goals you have developed for yourself.

Please do not do anything that would prevent you from coming to Texas. I need the visit as much as you do, and we both need the workshop that we will be attending.

Love you very much,
Your Khaki-Wearing Grandpa

Dear Khaki-Wearing Grandpa,

You had me giggling when you talked about a khaki-colored bikini. Then a package arrived, and in it was one of your old khaki shirts. I knew what the message was, and my father knew what the message was because he had read the draft of this chapter. The whole family had a good laugh and someone suggested that there was enough material for me to make a one-piece bathing suit rather than a bikini.

Knowing that I am being brought up like you were brought up makes it a little easier to bear the disappointment my father expresses, but I sure wish he would mix some approval in with that disappointment.

Why Do I Disappoint My Father?

Love you more,
Your Soon-to-Be-Khaki-Bikini-Clad Grand-
daughter

Grandpa's Note: *Seriously, when we see disappointment from a parent, it is usually because the parent can see the potential that we cannot see and thinks we need to be motivated. I know I did not see the potential that my parents saw in me.*

This chapter will be the lead chapter in the book Grandpa Help!— College, Careers, & Being Successful.. Check NordyBooks.com and GrandpaHelp.com for the publication date.

The next chapter, I'm Going to Give You a Kiss, falls into the category of being a teenager. It looks at the joys and feelings of being a teenager. Remember, your job description is to become independent. Your parents' job description is to keep you from killing yourself in the process. If both you and your parents are doing your jobs, there will be conflicts as well as joys.

Grandpa's Note: *At the conference, Paisly and I were each presented with a full scholarship to a three-day internet marketing conference in San Francisco. Due to my wife's surgery, I was not able to attend, but Paisly's father attended with her in my place. Without Paisly's hard work and enthusiasm, he would not have gone to this conference. As a result of the conference, a deal is developing that will provide*

Grandpa, Help!

consulting work for me, writing work for both Paisly and me, and additional work for Paisly's father. Paisly and her father also both caught the flu while at the conference. We suspect her father is so proud of her that he is about to pop the buttons on the front of his shirt, but he has not expressed it to her.

Why Do I Disappoint My Father?

Chapter 4 - Being a Teenager
I'm Going to Give You a Kiss

Grandpa,

You should have seen the expression on your face when I rushed into the room, slipped onto the couch next to you, wrapped my arms around you, puckered up, and announced so everyone in the room could hear, "I've always wanted to do this, so I'm going to give you a kiss." I had thought you would object, but you didn't. You seemed that you were very pleased that I was going to give you a kiss. I gave you a wonderful kiss. Was that the best kiss you ever had?

Love,
A Wet-Lipped Granddaughter

Dear Wet-Lipped,

You have the ability, like I have, to spin a story, tell the absolute truth, and give a completely wrong impression. This talent will serve you well as you become a much-sought-after writer and public speaker. Hopefully, that ability will not also send me to prison. To set

Grandpa, Help!

the record straight, so no one will think that I took advantage of you, I will record the "facts" as I remember them, or as I would like to remember them.

We were visiting friends at Coos Bay, Oregon. You and the other young people were downstairs while the adults were in the living room talking about adult things and checking email. There was a large bowl of candy kisses sitting on the coffee table. Periodically, each of us could not resist the temptation, and we would reach over and grab a kiss or two. Then a thundering herd came up the stairs with you in the lead. Each of you was wearing a big grin, so I knew something was up. You slipped onto the couch next to me and wrapped your arms around me. You puckered up ready for a kiss.

You looked deeply into my eyes. Then with a look of expectation on your face, you said, "Grandpa, I've always wanted to give you a kiss, so now I'm going to do it." You then removed your left arm from around me, opened up your hand, and held it between your lips and my lips, which at this point were at least twelve and a half inches apart. With both of us looking at that candy kiss in the palm of your hand, you said, "Enjoy."

You then stuck the candy kiss in my mouth and gave me one of those delicious hugs that you give. Later I found chocolate stains on the back of my shirt.

Meanwhile, your entourage was laughing and giggling, and the adults, even your mother and father, were thoroughly enjoying the byplay. I wonder, had

I'm Going to Give You a Kiss

you briefed them on what was coming so they would not rush in to save me from their conniving daughter?

I must make a confession; my daughter Dana was once sixteen. She has an imagination that is every bit as creative as yours. She once gave me a kiss, but I had to peel the aluminum foil off of it, and I did not get chocolate smeared on my shirt.

Now I have an assignment for you and your wonderful imagination. I need a 400-word article from you about what you would say to Judy, my lovely bride, if you had actually kissed me that evening.

We will keep our kisses to candy kisses, and hopefully we will never revert to my kissing your foot again. As you remember, that occurred when you had a thorn deeply imbedded in your foot, and you were hobbling around. The surgery caused me as much pain as it caused you, and I kissed your foot to make it well. If I remember your comment, you said that my kissing your foot made you feel like a princess and that I could do it as often as I wanted to.

Please, never put the child that lives within you away where she can't come out and play, because remaining a child at heart makes you who you are—a delightful person to know and associate with.

Love you even if you do smear chocolate on
my shirt,
Grandpa

Grandpa, Help!

This chapter will be the lead chapter in the book Grandpa Help!— Being a Teenager. Check NordyBooks.com and GrandpaHelp.com for the publication date. The teenage years contain a lot of stress, but they also are a time when a girl has a sparkle in her eyes as she goes out and has fun.

The next chapter, Why Can't I Hug a Hobo?, falls into the category of faith, religion, and ethics. It asks whether you can truly love a person or a group while keeping them at a distance.

I'm Going to Give You a Kiss

Chapter 5 - Faith, Religion, & Ethics
Why Can't I Hug a Hobo?

Abuelo,

I want to hug a hobo, but my parents are not very keen on it. I've served hobos in soup kitchens, but I've always had to keep my distance. Is it possible to love and care for your fellow man at a distance? You don't go around giving very many hugs, but it is very evident that you love people, that you care deeply for them, and that you work closely with them. So why don't you tell me how you can love people without giving them hugs and what you think of me wanting to hug a hobo?

I love humanity, it's people I cannot stand.
Just kidding, I think,
Nieta

Dearest Nieta,

Some years ago I wrote the following devotion after my dear friend, Alice, was appalled that she had hugged everyone else in our group but had not hugged

Grandpa, Help!

me, even though I had picked up the tab for her lunch. I wrote the devotion for fun, not in hopes of publication, but lo and behold, it was selected and published.

Have You Hugged Your Kayak Instructor Today?

Psalm 37:28-29 For the Lord loves justice; he will not forsake his saints. They are preserved forever, but the children of the wicked shall be cut off. The righteous shall inherit the land and dwell upon it forever. (ESV)

My father once told me that a man should never initiate a hug with a lady, because the lady might feel she was being mauled. He said that one did not get as many hugs that way, but the average hug was much better. I tried to follow this principle; but the non-verbal message I delivered must have been very clear, or my breath must really have been bad, because regularly, after hugging others, ladies would shake hands with me. Then I started having problems with some perfumes. A hug from the wrong lady would bring on a headache. When I started teaching deep-water re-entry in kayaks, the perfume problem got washed away.

I likened it to my sins being washed away with the blood of Jesus. So the question comes up, if your kayak instructor dunked you in the water

Why Can't I Hug a Hobo?

today and washed away your perfume and the set in your hair, so much so that you felt like a drowned rat, would you or could you respond with a hug?

Seriously, the hug I desire more than any other is from my Lord and Savior, Jesus Christ. Each time I study His Word, I receive such a hug. Actually, I'm enfolded in His arms at all times–it is just that sometimes I am not paying attention. In Matthew 28:20b, Jesus said, **"And behold, I am with you always, to the end of the age." (ESV)** *This is great comfort. Not only did Jesus pay the price for my sins, He is with me at all times.*

Lord, thank You for protecting me and comforting me, even when I forget to acknowledge that You are there caring for me. Amen.

That devotion sets the background for the way I give hugs. Raquel, a fellow kayaker, throws herself into giving hugs to people she likes. She hugs with so much enthusiasm, that I once asked her why Catholic ladies give so much better hugs than Lutheran ladies. Her immediate response was that Catholic ladies go to confession.

When we went to see the bats fly out from under Congress Street Bridge in Austin, we finished loading the kayaks at about 9:30 p.m. under a nearly full moon. As we finished, Raquel offered to arrange a

Grandpa, Help!

hugging contest, with me as the judge. I turned her down.

No, don't put me up on a pedestal for turning her down. I had a very good reason. I'd been up since 4:00 a.m., I had worked all day on a consulting job before going batty, I had the makings of a headache, and none of the ladies had fallen in the water, so some smelled rather rankly of perfume. If I had participated, I would have had a full-blown headache before I got halfway home, and I would have had to pull off the road and sleep it off. Besides, I was too tired to have thrown myself into such a contest.

When Rev. Tilt was in seminary, he had a class that required him to interview Christians about what they would look for in a church if they were in a town that did not have a Lutheran Church. He asked me that question, and I responded with a comment my father had made about the Catholic Church having such beautiful music that he might become Catholic. The next day I responded that Catholic ladies gave wonderful hugs, so that would be a reason to go to a Catholic Church. The third day I responded that I would look for a church that preached the Gospel and was working. While I do not know which of the responses Rev. Tilt actually used, he told me that he was going to use the one about hugs.

You once told me about a church member who went around demanding hugs because he needed them. You also mentioned that many ladies tended to avoid him so he could not demand a hug from them. I

Why Can't I Hug a Hobo?

suspect that hugs that are demanded are nowhere near as good as those that are freely given.

Christ freely gave Himself on the Cross to save us. He also associated with sinners and even went into their homes and ate with them. I do not know of a Bible verse that says that Jesus hugged those whom the Pharisees considered to be "The Great Unwashed," but from other things written about Him, I suspect He would have had no problem hugging a hobo. Meanwhile, your parents are following a tradition that they learned from their parents of keeping a certain distance while helping people. If you get too close to some people who need help, they can become very demanding. It is much easier for a person to keep a little distance while helping others. Is it wrong to keep a distance while helping others? NO! Is hugging a hobo wrong? NO! Explain your position to your parents, and then go hug a hobo.

Are you going to select a gorgeous hobo to hug or one with rotten teeth who smells of stale tobacco smoke? Are you going to hug one, or are you going to hug twenty? Can you give the twentieth one as good of a hug as you gave the first one?

Remember, every action has consequences. Consider the consequences of whatever decision you make, and make sure you are able to live with them. What is the worst thing that could happen if you hugged a hobo? Is it that you might end up falling in love with one and marrying him? Then you would be a hobo, and you could go to soup kitchens and have your

Grandpa, Help!

parents feed you. Are you giggling now? Seriously, talk the reasons and consequences over with your parents, and maybe they will join you in hugging a hobo.

Amor siempre,
Abuelo

This chapter will be the lead chapter in the book Grandpa Help!— Faith, Religion, & Ethics. Check NordyBooks.com and Grandpa-Help.com for the publication date.

The next chapter, I've Been Mauled by Love, belongs to the category of other relationships. These are the relationships that fall outside the categories of dating and parental relationships. This chapter explores the special languages and key words that develop between people. It is a fun read. Picture how I felt when my granddaughter screamed, "He's mauling me!" at the top of her voice when I put my arms around her to give her a hug. Think about how her parents reacted. You will learn why she did not consider being mauled to be a bad thing.

Why Can't I Hug a Hobo?

Chapter 6 - Other Relationships
I've Been Mauled by Love

Abuelo,

You sent me a draft of the devotion, and asked if it was reasonably accurate. I thought it was, so I read it aloud to my family. They enjoyed it very much. I could barely read it, though, because I was constantly on the verge of giggling. No, I was giggling most of the time I was reading it.

All of us have an idea about what mauling is, but you have given it an entirely different meaning. You should have seen the expression on your face that day when I screamed, "He's mauling me. He really cares." I wish that I had had my camera to record it. My whole family agrees that you can maul each and every one of us whenever you choose.

Since my family approves of your mauling, I guess you could say that I am a trendsetter. Now everyone enjoys being mauled by you. Part of it might be because of how infrequently you maul others. It's kind of like if you had chocolates only once a year. HOW SAD.

Grandpa, Help!

54

Maybe you should change your standards and make it a point to give more hugs, rather than waiting until someone finally gets the urge to hug you.

> *I'm mauling you with love.*
> *Please maul me back,*
> *Nieta*

Grandpa's Note: *Here is the devotion that Nieta was referring to. My wife, Judy, and I are involved in writing and publishing devotions for our church. Periodically, I will insert a devotion to illustrate a point.*

Key Words

Luke 2:6-7 And while they were there, the time came for her to give birth. And she gave birth to her firstborn son and wrapped him in swaddling cloths and laid him in a manger, because there was no place for them in the inn. (ESV)

"He's mauling me. He really cares." These words came from my granddaughter's lips and rang through the motor home park as I gave her a hug. Needless to say, we had some explaining to do. A week before, I had told her that I do not go around initiating hugs with ladies because I would not want them to feel as if they were being mauled. She assured me that I could maul her anytime I wanted to. I wonder where she got her weird sense of humor. When I saw she needed a

I've Been Mauled By Love

hug that Friday afternoon, I initiated one. Mauling her was the furthest thing from my mind. After the explanation, her entire family assured me that I could maul each of them whenever I chose.

Some words and phrases carry special significance. There are now a few people for whom the word "maul" brings on an entirely different meaning than it does for the general population. As Christians, we also have key words and phrases that have special meaning to us. These include words like "manger" and "cross." They are key words that remind us of the forgiveness of sins and salvation that God has provided for us. Unless we tell non-Christians the meaning of these words, they may never learn their significance and the love that they describe. If I can explain to my fifteen-year-old granddaughter's mother that mauling her daughter is a good thing, could explaining the manger and the cross to a friend be impossible?

Lord, help me to open my mouth and my heart so I can explain to all of my friends why words like manger and cross have such a deep meaning in my life. Amen.

Dearest Nieta,

My friend Gail saw the devotion about mauling. After the kayaking class yesterday, she came up to me

Grandpa, Help!

and said, "I want you to maul me." You are a trendsetter.

> *Te Amo,*
> *Abuelo*

Abuelo and Haleigh,

I've been taking a nap, and you guys have been aw-
fully quiet. When you talk between yourselves and I'm
left out, I always wonder what you're saying about me.
Are you talking about me? If you have been, I hope you
have been saying nice things.

> *Te Amo,*
> *Nieta*

Nieta,

We were saying what a wonderful and loveable
person you are, but that we would hate for you to
realize that is what we think, because it might go to
your head. Now, consider yourself mauled.

> *Te Amo,*
> *Abuelo*

Abuelo,

Mauled with yours and Haleigh's love? I don't
think I could find anything better. All of your talking
has already gone to my head. So feel free to say even
more nice things about me. It's too late, anyway. Do I

I've Been Mauled By Love

have that cheesy granddaughter thing down adequately?

I am mauled by your love,
Nieta

Nieta,

Just when I know how much you love me, you throw a comment in about that "cheesy granddaughter thing." This is one of the things that makes the bond between us so strong. Even while being serious, either one of us can throw a zinger in, and the other automatically sees the positive intention behind it. This makes having you as my granddaughter fun. With others, we often need to be careful about making comments like that, because they may not see our words in the positive manner that we intend. This is part of what makes relationships messy.

I promised you several years ago that I would answer your questions and be very honest with you. This has worked out very well, even though you have had me sweating several times. Recently, when we were at a writing conference, you asked if I thought an outfit was appropriate. I responded that it was. A few minutes later, as we were walking down the hall, I saw a flash of white and momentarily thought it was your underwear showing. It was actually the undershirt you were wearing and within a second or two I recognized what it was, your undershirt. Since we had talked about the appropriateness of your outfit a few minutes

Grandpa, Help!

before, I mentioned my mistaken impression. You responded with a grin and a hug. If your father had made the same comment, he probably would not have gotten a grin and a hug. It is always a good idea to taste our words before we speak them, because many people inadvertently put a spin on what they hear or read. As a result, they receive something that is different than we intended.

Now, I must confess that I think that your hugs are a work of art, and I welcome you to maul me anytime you are around. Why don't you hop on a plane and come see me this afternoon?

Relationships are fun, but they can be messy.

Te Amo,
Abuelo

This chapter will be the lead chapter in the book Grandpa Help!— Other Relationships. Check NordyBooks.com and GrandpaHelp.com for the publication date.

The next chapter, Should Divorced Parents Date?, falls into the category of relationships with your parents. As you read it, remember, no matter how awkward you may feel when a parent begins to date, your parents have feelings, too. Being respectful of their romantic relationships will make this difficult time a little easier for everyone involved.

I've Been Mauled By Love

Chapter 7 - The Parents
Should Divorced Parents Date?

Dear Grandpa,

Is it normal for divorced parents to date? Yes, I know it is, but should I have so many mixed emotions about it? Should I like the guys my mother dates? When I don't like them, how should I treat them? When I do like them, how should I treat them?

Your confused granddaughter,
Jessica

Dear Jessica,

The answers to your questions are yes, yes, not necessarily, politely, and politely. Should I leave it there, or should we proceed?

Strange as it may seem, parents are people. People like to have relationships with other people. That includes relationships with people of the opposite sex. Some of those relationships are platonic, while others have a romantic side to them. This leads to dating.

Grandpa, Help!

Remember, just as you want to be in a relationship, many single adults also want to be in relationships. This is part of being human. While it is easy to understand on an intellectual level that a parent may be romantically interested in another single adult, it is often difficult to accept this on a heart level. Additional problems develop if the parents have recently divorced or if the child fears that she somehow caused the divorce. The child may also worry about losing the parent's love when the parent begins a new relationship.

When a relationship ends, oftentimes the root cause of the breakup will carry forward into new relationships. This leads to serial breakups. Now I am going to ask you to put on a tight shoe and see how much it hurts. You learned about relationships from your parents. If their relationships were not solid, are you going to repeat their mistakes in your own relationships? If not, how are you going to develop a new pattern to follow?

When considering the cause of a breakup, look beneath the surface. If parents fight about disciplining their children, the underlying issue may be a power struggle. Who makes the decisions in their relationship? If the couple did not have children, they might be fighting over whether to buy a four-wheel-drive pickup or a shocking pink sports car. If couples do not realize what their real issues are, how can they address and resolve them? If your parents did not figure out their

Should Divorced Parents Date?

real issues, you may have difficulty recognizing the real issues in your own relationships.

On the other end of the spectrum, parents who have watched their own children grow up, get married, have children, get divorced, and then start dating again, experience many of the same emotions as their teenaged grandchildren. It might be appropriate for the grandchildren and the grandparents to sit down and talk about the things that are difficult for all of them.

When a parent dates, you see things that the parent doesn't see. Just like the parent sees things that you don't see. It's almost as if the person that the parent is dating is not the same person that you see. If I were a psychologist, which thankfully I am not, I would be talking about viewing the boyfriends or girlfriends through different lenses. This would be difficult for me, since I have only one pair of glasses.

We all have the tendency to create a vision of our ideal mate. When we meet someone and consider dating them, we sometimes impose that vision on the "victim" of our interest. Since the "victim" seldom lives up to the vision, most relationships do not develop. If they do develop, many fail when we see the "victim's" actual characteristics.

In like manner, most teenagers have a vision of what sort of person their parent should bring home. Without ever realizing it, the date is just as much a victim of your vision as he is of your mother's vision.

Grandpa, Help!

Feel sorry for him, since he has been doubly victimized.

It is very natural for a person who goes through a divorce, to be interested in developing another relationship. Some start to date before the divorce is final; others wait for a number of years before dating again. Then there are those who start dating before the divorce has even been discussed. We will not discuss those individuals in this chapter.

After a divorce, some people end up dating a person who is very similar to their ex-spouse. Others don't want to make the same mistake again, so they date people who are extremely different. Often the teenaged daughter can see this better than the parent can. Unless a person understands why their divorce really happened, their next relationship may suffer the same fate as the first.

One computer dating service advertises on TV that they check 29 points of compatibility when matching people. I have no idea whether they actually do this or whether the 29 points of compatibility are enough. I suspect that when filling out the application forms, most people indulge in a little wishful thinking.

Even if you make it a point to get to know the new boyfriend or girlfriend, and get to like him or her, your parent may still end the relationship. This wouldn't happen because of something you did, but because they could not see a long-term relationship going forward. Be careful. You do not need to be hurt any more.

Should Divorced Parents Date?

Sometimes the new boyfriend or girlfriend figures that the way to impress their date is to be really nice to any children and get them on their side. Others prefer to ignore children, almost as if they are hoping the children will go away. Either approach makes for an awkward situation. It is very difficult for you to really like someone in these circumstances.

Then we come to the rules and regulations related to dating. Your parent may tell you that if you're going out on a date, you have to be home by ten. But your parent doesn't come home until well after midnight. That seems like a double standard. Frankly, it is, but the parent usually makes the rules, and the child is expected to obey them.

An even stickier situation develops when it comes to sleeping over. Do your parents ever let your boyfriend sleep over? Can you picture the reaction if you asked if he could? But the parent, without seeing any problem, may allow his/her own date to do so. Or you may end up meeting the new boyfriend or girlfriend coming out of the bathroom when you are getting ready for school. Do I need to suggest that this is a very awkward situation? In the parents' defense, they often assume that you will not realize what is going on. Then to make matters worse, when you point out what you have seen and what you have figured out, you get a lecture on not having sex before you get married. That is an even more awkward situation.

Would you prefer for your mom to sit down with you before she goes out on a date and tell you that she

Grandpa, Help!

expects to bring her date home for the night because she needs to have sex and needs to feel like she is desirable? If that happens, no matter what you say, it will be wrong. So you might as well just say, "Take precautions so you don't catch something." Can you picture telling your parent that?

A better option would be to mention the book *Success Before Sex* and state that reading it would help the two of you communicate. Then she would read it in order to understand you better and inadvertently she would learn about all of the problems connected to sex outside of marriage.

What you do not want to point out is that she says she needs sex, but that you are being told that you should abstain. That will only lead to an argument, and as you know, I contend that no one ever wins an argument. It just damages a relationship.

It is easy to look at a parent's life, or for that matter, the life of anyone you know well, and see where they have made major blunders. At some point you may be in a similar position and make major blunders, too. Periodically, I mention that I'm thinking about running as a write-in candidate for the office of the President of the United States of America. My platform would be that I will not make the mistakes that Obama made, or that either Bush made, or that Clinton made, or any that other president made. I will make a whole bunch of my own very unique mistakes. That is what every parent goes through, and having a child point

Should Divorced Parents Date?

out their mistakes is one of the things that dating parents dread.

Are you familiar with the powdered butt syndrome? A person will never take unsolicited advice from a person whose butt she/he powdered. They just are not programmed to listen to any advice you may offer.

Yes, parents are going to date. When you meet the date, be polite. Then try to excuse yourself so you are not causing an already awkward situation to be even more awkward for them. Try to treat the date like you would like to be treated. Not easy; and frankly, there are no good answers for you.

I wish I could offer more help.

You have my sympathy and prayers,
Grandpa

This chapter will be the lead chapter in the book Grandpa Help!— The Parents. Check Nordy-Books.com and GrandpaHelp.com for the publication date.

The next chapter, What is Vulgarity?, falls into the category of drugs, alcohol, cursing, swearing, and vulgarity. As you read it, remember that vulgar terms have meanings, and that if you use them, you may be saying things that you never intended to say. What would you do if someone took you literally, and you had to beg them to understand that you did not know what you were saying? You probably could not convince them that you did not know what

Grandpa, Help!

you were saying. Even if you could, you would lose face, and you do not want to do that.

Should Divorced Parents Date?

Chapter 8 - Drugs, Alcohol, Cursing, Swearing, & Vulgarity
What Is Vulgarity?

Grandpa,

I used the F- word the other day. Uncle Pete took exception to it and told me that I should have my mouth washed out with soap. What is wrong with using it? Everyone does. Well, nearly everyone. I don't remember you or Uncle Pete ever using it, but I don't know why you two are the only people in the world who don't. Everyone else I know uses it regularly. A person has to use it to fit in with friends.

By the way, soap tastes awful, so I don't want Uncle Pete to wash my mouth out with soap for using a perfectly good word that everyone uses. Who ever came up with the idea of washing a mouth out with soap? It does not remove the words, even if they were bad.

Love,
Your Cutest Granddaughter

Grandpa, Help!

Dear Cutest,

You might be surprised at the number of people who never use the F- word. Over the years, I've heard you use a few words that I don't use. Do you know what some of those words actually mean? I'd like to take a little time and talk to you about what you're actually saying when you use them.

First, vulgarity is normally considered to be the use of crude words when much better words are available. Even though Haleigh does not see a difference between cursing and vulgarity, there is a major difference. Cursing is asking our Lord to send someone or something to Hell.

Let's start at the top. Have you ever used the F- word? Before you deny it, remember that you have used it in my presence. Go back and read your question where you admitted using it. Do you really know what the F- word signifies?

The F- word refers to sexual intercourse. Often it refers to nonconsensual sexual intercourse or rape. So when you get irritated at your boyfriend and you say "F- you," you're saying that you want to have sexual intercourse with him. You are saying you would rape him if he does not want to be cooperative. What would you do if he responded, "Fine, let's do it now"? He has every right to respond in that manner, since you are proposing having sexual intercourse with him.

However, the expression is slung around so much that he may not react when you use it. What do you mean when you say the F- word? Are you merely using

What Is Vulgarity?

it to fill in a gap in the conversation because you are not bright enough to think of another word? That is why many people use it. Besides being cute, you are also bright, so you cannot get away with using that as an excuse.

Now that you know what the expression really means, are you likely to use it as often as you have in the past? I suspect that there are some young ladies out there who use the word and mean exactly what it says, but they probably aren't reading this book.

How many times have you said the F- word followed by "yourself"? You know you're telling the person to do something that is not possible. Is that polite of you? Do you think the victim of your "wit" should get irritated?

You probably use these words with people other than your boyfriend. In fact, you might use them more often with other people. What if you said the F- word to a teacher and the teacher had the principal announce over the intercom that you had suggested sexual intercourse? You would be the talk of the school. You are probably safe from this, because most principals are very politically correct.

Vulgarities are regularly used among friends, but do you really want to make suggestions like these to the people you are close to? What I would like for you to do is pause before you use the F- word. Take just a moment and consider whether it really means what you are trying to express. If it does, then I suggest that you get ready to catch a sexually-transmitted disease

Grandpa, Help!

or become pregnant. The odds will be stacked against you if you participate in that much sexual activity with that many partners.

Then there is the word "screw." A screw is a device that is used to join two substances together. The word has also become a slang term for sexual intercourse. So if you say, "S- you," to someone, you are actually proposing sexual intercourse.

You probably know a lot of people who use vulgarity because they want to impress their friends. Is your best girlfriend going to be impressed if you say you want to have sexual intercourse with her? What about your parents? What thoughts will you have now when somebody says these words to you? Hopefully, you're going to quit using them and be an example who leads your friends to stop, too. Will it be easy? NO!

To taper off, start by counting the number of times you use these words each day. You will probably be surprised at how prolific you are in vulgarity. Once you are aware of how frequently you use the words, you can start deliberately cutting back. While you are doing this, ask yourself how long it will take your friends to notice a change in you. If you want their support, offer to pay them a nickel every time you use one of the words.

It may be easier than you think. For years men used these terms when they were around other men, but they would not think of using them when they were around women. This indicates to me that vulgarity is a conscious decision. It also indicates that the feminist

What Is Vulgarity?

movement had some results that not all women welcome.

There are other vulgar terms that are not quite as explicit as the ones we have been discussing. Recently, I quit using the phrase "pissed off." I used it once in front of your cousin Haleigh, and she chewed me out. I pointed out that I had heard her use it. She countered that it was okay for her, but it was not okay for her favorite grandfather to use it. I eliminated the term from my vocabulary, and I will probably be chided for even writing it down in this book. Meanwhile, I maintain that a double standard is being imposed on me. I cannot use words that my granddaughter throws around all the time.

The other day Haleigh's mother needed to borrow an air mattress. I put it in the trunk of my car, then met Haleigh and her mother at a restaurant. I opened the trunk from inside the car and went around back to get it out. The mattress was not there. I started to say "Oh, shoot." I got as far as the S and stopped. Haleigh was horrified, believing that I had started to say "Oh, shit." She will not even begin to acknowledge that I intended to say, "Oh, shoot." Now I'm guilty, even though I didn't say the word that she uses regularly. To keep me from being caught in this double standard, will you help Haleigh improve her choice of words? Good luck!

You've met the famous author Tucker Max. In fact, you've been in the room with him when he used the F-word probably fifteen times in ten minutes. Did he

Grandpa, Help!

impress you as somebody you would like to spend time with? He has it all. He's a multimillionaire. He's athletic. He's a beer drinker. He chases women. And he has about the foulest mouth I have ever encountered. Please don't pattern your conversations after Tucker Max. Maybe each time I hear you use the F- word, I should call you Tucker.

You recently told me that you picked up one of his books in a bookstore and scanned a few pages. In the book, his language is cleaner, but the book was still not something that you figured I would approve of you reading. Since you did not buy the book, maybe you did not approve of it either. See, you are making progress already.

If you really want to make an impression on someone, you can be creative. My father told a story about my mother. My parents didn't own a lawnmower, so my father trimmed the front yard with a Swing Blade. In this day and time, few people know what a Swing Blade is. Picture it as a muscle-powered weed trimmer. It has a blade about fifteen inches long that is sharpened on each edge. The blade is attached to a handle, and it cuts grass and weeds when it is swung back and forth a few inches above the ground. It gets the job done, but it doesn't do it nice and neat like a lawnmower does.

This was in the days before they had gas-powered lawnmowers. The only type of lawnmower available was a push-powered, reel-type lawnmower. It pro-

What Is Vulgarity?

duced a beautifully smooth cut, and it could cut as close to the ground or as high up as you wanted.

A salesman showed up one day and pushed his demonstration lawnmower diagonally across the front yard and up to my parents' front doorstep. It cut a beautiful swath that stood out like a sore thumb against the rest of the lawn. The salesman knocked on the door and proceeded to try to hard-sell my mother into buying a lawnmower. He wanted $12.95. That was a high price back in the 1930s when this happened. My mother was not happy. It would take weeks before the swath he had cut would disappear. However, she didn't use the F- word. She didn't use the S- word either. She looked at him, smiled, and said, "Young man, I hope your mother doesn't come out from under the porch and bite you." Do you know what she called him without using any off-color words? He knew. His mouth dropped open, his face turned kind of pale, and he left. A bitch is a female dog. Back then many front porches were raised above the soil, and the cool space beneath was a favorite spot for dogs. My mother very effectively called the salesman a son of a bitch with a sweet smile on her face and without ever raising her voice.

Back when I was a kid, I often heard the term "fiddlesticks." It was used in place of a curse word or vulgarity, but no one ever confused it with a curse word or vulgarity.

A famous author once said, "Beauty is in the eye of the beholder, and cute is in the words she chooses to

Grandpa, Help!

use." Based on that statement, I know how you can be even cuter. I just remembered; I am that famous author.

> *Love you,*
> *even if you are foul-mouthed,*
> *Grandpa*

This chapter will be the lead chapter in the book Grandpa Help!— Drugs, Alcohol, Cursing, Swearing, & Vulgarity. Check Nordy-Books.com and GrandpaHelp.com for the publication date.

The next chapter, Adam vs. Eve, falls into the marriage category. What do you think of polygamy? As you read this chapter, remember that studies show that fifty percent of marriages break up. Among those under twenty years of age, the failure rate is even higher. When a high remarriage rate is factored in, this leads to a condition known as serial polygamy.

What Is Vulgarity?

Chapter 9 - Marrying & Marriage
Adam vs. Eve

Grandpa,

Why did Eve eat the apple in the Garden of Eden and mess it up for all of us who would not have listened to that old snake? Men are usually the ones who mess up, and then women are blamed when things go wrong. Why couldn't Adam have been the one to listen to the snake and eat the apple? Is it possible he did, but that men passed the story down to Moses, and Moses just wrote what he had been told? Maybe the lesson that we should take from Adam and Eve is that when a marriage is going well, one of the partners is going to mess it up. That partner is usually the man.

I'm in a snake-killing mood,
Thoroughly Modern Eve

Dear Docile, Little Eve,

You have met my friend Ann. We went to school together, and I ruined her brand-new saddle oxfords.

Grandpa, Help!

That was over fifty years ago, and I am still paying. When the time is ripe, I'll tell you the story. Ann has found that as the nights get cooler, when she opens her garage door in the morning, she regularly finds a rattlesnake lying just under the lip of the door trying to absorb some heat from inside the garage. She has learned to kill the rattlesnake with a hoe. One chop is all it takes. Then one bad rattlesnake becomes two good rattlesnakes. Ann used to use a shotgun, but with trying to maneuver so she did not hit the wrong thing (such as her car) with ricochets, sometimes the rattlesnake would get away, or worse, head into the garage and find valuable possessions (read junk) to hide behind while Ann remained on the warpath. If Eve had been like Ann, and had a hoe handy, the entire story would have been different.

Most of us know the story of Adam and Eve, but since a few may not, I'd like to briefly review it. Then I'll give my interpretation. When I'm through, you're going to look at Adam and Eve a little differently than you did before. In **Genesis 1:1** we read that God created the heavens and the earth. As we continue reading, we learn the details of the creation story and how humankind fell into sin. In six days God created the heavens and the earth, including man. He said all of it was good, and on the seventh day He rested. He named the first man Adam.

The word Adam comes from a Hebrew word meaning red earth. Therefore, I believe that Adam had red hair, because if you're created from the dust of the earth out of red dirt, aren't you going to have red hair? He probably had freckles, also.

Adam was alone. Yes, he had the animals, but there was no one of his own kind. So God put him into a deep sleep, took a rib, and created Eve. Eve probably had red hair and freckles, too, since she was made from one of Adam's ribs. Eve was to be a helpmate for Adam. You could say that Adam was in charge, and Eve was his helper.

There are people who claim that the account in Genesis could not be real, since men have the same number of ribs as women. That is faulty thinking. If a man has an arm cut off, will all of his progeny be born missing an arm? Of course not. If a rib was removed to make Eve, Adam would have a missing rib, but his progeny would still have the normal complement of ribs.

Adam and Eve were happy in the Garden of Eden where God had placed them, and God had told them that they could eat of any tree in the garden except the Tree of the Knowledge of Good and Evil. Then one day, while they were wandering around the garden, a serpent spoke to Eve. **Genesis 3:1** uses the pronoun "he" for the serpent. Does that mean that the serpent, who was actually Satan in the form of a serpent, was a male and, in typical male fashion, was tempting a young lady? The other possibility is that the pronoun "he" could have referred to either a male or a female. That was common for many years, but I digress.

Grandpa, Help!

The serpent questioned Eve about God's instructions. Eve listened, and ultimately the serpent convinced Eve that the fruit of the Tree of the Knowledge of Good and Evil was good to eat. He promised it would even help her to become like God, knowing the difference between good and evil. Eve took a bite of the fruit. The Bible does not identify the fruit as an apple, but many artists have.

Eve found it was good and turned to her husband, Adam, who was right there with her. She handed it to him and said, "Try it. You'll like it." He did. Suddenly, they realized what they hadn't noticed before: they were naked. So they took fig leaves and sewed them together to make clothes.

This part of the story has always bothered me. I am allergic to fig leaves, and if I am around them for a while, my skin starts burning. I wonder, did the fig leaves affect <u>them</u> in a similar way?

Anyway, God came walking in the garden that evening and asked Adam why he and Eve were hiding. Adam responded that they were hiding because they were naked. God asked if they had eaten from the Tree of the Knowledge of Good and Evil. Adam didn't say yes. Instead he said, "That woman that You made from my rib and gave to me as my helper ate from the tree. Then she gave some fruit to me. What was I supposed to do? If I hadn't eaten it, we would have had an awful argument. This is all her fault and Your fault."

Adam vs. Eve

As a result of Adam blaming Eve, in every generation since, husbands have blamed their wives whenever the husband messes up.

If we look at what scripture actually says, we find a slightly different story than the one Adam told. Adam was with Eve when the serpent tempted Eve. After Eve ate, she turned to Adam and gave him some of the fruit.

Consider who is at fault if you are working beside your boss and you give a customer the wrong information, but your boss does not say anything. Yes, Eve gave in to temptation, but Adam kept his mouth shut and enjoyed the fruit, too, until God confronted him. Adam was guiltier than Eve. All Adam would have had to do was give Eve a hug and say to the serpent, "We are not interested."

Eve needed a good press agent. Instead she allowed her loving husband to be in charge of public relations. He threw her under the bus. Ever since, the world has held her responsible, when Adam should have been carrying most of the blame.

One of these days you're going to get married. Do you want a relationship like Adam and Eve had, or do you want one that's based on truth? A lot depends on the decisions you make when selecting a spouse.

I hope this helps you understand that life is not always fair, even when dealing with a loving husband. I believe Adam should have shouldered most of the blame for man's fall, but I do not foresee my opinion being commonly accepted.

Grandpa, Help!

Remember, many snakes walk on two legs, and some of them are going to propose marriage to you. Next time you come to Texas, maybe you would like to spend some time with Ann and learn some snake-killing techniques from her.

Love,
Grandpa

This chapter will be the lead chapter in the book Grandpa Help!— Marrying & Marriage. Check NordyBooks.com and Grandpa-Help.com for the publication date.

The next chapter, What Do I Want to Do With My Life?, falls into the category of dreams, visions, passions, and goals. As you read it, remember that if you have not decided where you want to go in life, you may not go anywhere at all. Many people will tell you which direction you should go, but often they are really just telling you what you should be doing to help them reach their own goals. You need to determine where you want to go in your life, and then follow your own dreams.

Adam vs. Eve

Chapter 10 - Dreams, Visions, Passions, & Goals
What Do I Want to Do with My Life?

Grandpa,

There are so many things that I can do and do well. I'm an excellent photographer and a very good writer. I've developed websites, and I've also Search Engine Optimized a number of websites. I can lead nature walks, and when people are feeling down, I can counsel them and help them feel better. With all that I do well, I'm having problems deciding which things to focus on. I know I want to be an entrepreneur, but what kind of entrepreneur? I know I want to help people, but what kind of help do I want to provide? What groups of people do I want to help? My sister, Suzie, is three years younger than me and already knows what she wants to focus on. My brother, Bobby, is two years younger than me, and he knows, too. You know that boys are always slower than girls, but he has already decided, and I have not.

Grandpa, Help!

I know that you have done a number of things in your life. There are people who claim you are a world-class expert in several areas. Can you tell me what I really want to do? Other people tell me what I should be doing, but they are telling me things that fit in with their goals and ambitions. Maybe I should have asked, "How do I decide where my focus should be?"

Your granddaughter with a tremendous amount of potential,
Paisly

Dearest Paisly,

Are you sure that you want to ask me this question?

The word that jumps out in your letter is "potential." In the military, if an officer is rated as having potential, as opposed to actually having accomplished something, it may ruin his career. It screams to the command structure that he has ability that he is not using. Talent and potential are two very overrated qualities. Neither one will get you very far if you are not motivated.

I started out working in a brick plant and a pozzolan plant and worked my way up to Assistant to the Head of Research and Development. Then I spent a bit of time catching rattlesnakes to pay school expenses. While it was fun and rewarding, I would not recommend that you catch rattlesnakes for a living. The military trained me in photography and sent me on an all-expenses-paid tour of Southeast Asia to practice my

What Do I Want to Do with My Life?

combat photography skills. For several years I was a chemistry teacher. I worked for the Texas Water Quality Board as a hydrologist, while trying to make a name for myself as a landscape photographer. Then I ran a mining operation in Arizona. I later became the president of a company that manufactured colored cements and stuccos here in Texas. Meanwhile, I imported minerals from Mexico and sold them. Then I harvested mesquite and sold mesquite lumber via mail order. I also made items from mesquite lumber, ranging from Christmas ornaments to rocking chairs and briefcases. I worked in research and development in cements and pozzolans. After getting fired, I set up a consulting firm that solves cement-related problems on buildings all over the U.S. Additionally, I am a writer. I write construction books and books with life lessons. On top of all of that, I am a wilderness kayaking guide.

If you follow the textbook guidance, it will tell you that you need to focus on one item early on and become an expert in that area. Obviously, even though I have become an expert in several areas, I haven't focused on one. Looking over what I have done, I guess deep down I was an entrepreneur, even though I never learned how to spell the word, and I always wanted the safety net of a full-time job. Getting fired (they called it a layoff) was one of the best things that ever happened to me.

If I had focused on catching and selling rattlesnakes, I probably would have ended up like my

Grandpa, Help!

partner in the rattlesnake venture. He got bit a number of times. Once when he got bit, he asked his wife to use the shotgun and shoot his thumb off so the pain would go away. If I had taken that career path, would we have ever met?

As you develop into an entrepreneur, if you can focus on your current project(s) rather than looking for a safety net, you will have a much greater chance of success. Also remember, like the Apostle Paul, to be happy in whatever circumstances you find yourself. You will have times when you will have more money than you can spend. You will have times when you have to hunt on the sidewalk to find two pennies to rub together.

When my daughter, Dana, was going to school, she told me that she wanted to have a general enough education so that if she changed her direction in life, she would be prepared. Dana has an advanced degree in wildlife management, and she currently owns a Montessori school with approximately eighty students. I guess you could say that controlling eighty students falls under the category of Wildlife Management.

As you go through life, everything around you changes. You should be prepared to change, too. When people put too much emphasis on focusing, I like to mention that I still have stock in a buggy whip company, and I fully expect horse-drawn carriages to come back into vogue. This, of course, is tongue-in-cheek, but it illustrates that a once-thriving industry no longer exists. Unemployment statistics show that many of the chronically unemployed are unemployed because their skill set is no longer needed. These workers have not been motivated to learn a new set of skills and possibly accept employment at a lower wage.

When I was a kid, we didn't have the Internet. My brother built a crystal set so we could listen to the radio. He even talked about building crystal sets and selling them. When I was in graduate school (don't tell anyone, because no one is supposed to know that I have more than an eighth-grade education), very simple computers took up entire rooms and required massive air conditioners to keep them from overheating. The laptop that you complain is too slow can do many times more work than those room-sized machines. Key punching was a hot field then, too, and every manager had at least one secretary who took shorthand. We didn't even have Facebook, Amazon.com, or iPhones. By the time you have teenaged children, many of the technologies that seem essential to your current life may be obsolete. Yes, you need a focus; but, more importantly, you need to know how to think and how to reach out and grasp opportunities.

Going to college is not necessarily the answer. My Uncle Carrol had seven children, and he put each one through college. He used to comment that we needed more high school dropouts. Someone would always ask him why, and he would respond, "We need someone to hire all of these college graduates." He believed, and there is a lot of truth in his belief, that most people who go to college learn what will not work, not how to

Grandpa, Help!

think and overcome obstacles. The high school drop-out does not realize that conventional wisdom says that certain things will not work, so she tries them out and finds ways to make them work. Carrol regularly pointed out that high school dropouts were much more prominent among the super-rich than among the general population.

Another way of looking at it is that a college education teaches you how to get a job and work for someone else. That includes prestigious business schools. A Harvard MBA simply teaches you how to work for a bigger company, not how to be an entrepreneur.

If you want to be an entrepreneur, you need some type of education, not necessarily in a classroom, besides a college education. Possibly you need to start several small business, like your sister and her rabbits. Several failures will teach you a great deal. Put your last dime into each business, but do not borrow money. You will be motivated to learn if your next meal depends on it. This will also teach you how to start a business on a shoestring.

As a first step in deciding what you want to do with your life, and of course this is only a first step, I would suggest that you start thinking about what your passions are. What (besides gorgeous boys) causes you to get excited?

You have indicated that you want to help people. Helping people can lead you to a career as a nurse, a doctor, or a child protective services caseworker; or

What Do I Want to Do with My Life?

you could become somebody like Bill Gates who made a fortune and then used much of it to help others. Just because you own a company that is dedicated to making a profit, doesn't mean that you can't help people. This is where your interest in being an entrepreneur can really shine.

Currently, you are a co-author of this series of books, along with Haleigh and me. You are handling, among other things, the promotion of the book through the Internet and building and maintaining the website. Do you love doing that? If you do, you might want to continue doing this sort of work. You love to take pictures, and about two years ago you thought you would like to be a photographer. Now, you don't want to be just a photographer, but you wouldn't mind being in a field where you could utilize both photography and your design skills to help people.

So, I would suggest that you get out a couple sheets of paper. That goes back to my upbringing, when we put things down on paper. You may prefer to use a computer. But whatever method you choose, you can get started by dividing your document into several sections. One section should be occupation. The second section should be education; the third, spouse; the fourth, children; and the fifth, home and where your home will be located.

Then you can start filling in each section. Dream big. Don't worry if others think your dreams are crazy. The fellow who started FedEx proposed the concept during a class he was taking in business school. His

Grandpa, Help!

professor told him that it was impractical. How many times do you use that impractical concept each month? Remember, at this point you are brainstorming. You can refine your vision later.

You could come up with a vision that says, "I will buy Grandpa's buggy whip stock for one dollar and other outstanding shares for similar amounts. That will give me control of a buggy whip company. I will make the best buggy whips available, and I will build the company into a major corporation. With the profits, I will set up a foundation that ships the food that American children do not want to eat to places in the world where children are starving. I will prepare for this career by attending school through the eighth grade. I will marry a strong Christian man who shares my political beliefs, has an eighth-grade education, and supports my wild ideas. We will be normal Americans, and we will have 2 5/8 children. We will make our home in a castle sitting on a mountaintop on the beach in Waikiki, Hawaii."

I hope you're giggling by this time. What I want to stress is that you need to figure out what is important to you as you develop your vision for your life. If you don't, then someone (like me) will take your hand, look deeply into your eyes, and say, "Paisly, you need to go to work for me and make me successful." While I would love to have you as a partner in producing and marketing books, that might not be your vision. It might be a step toward your vision, though, as you learn writing and publishing processes. I spent many

What Do I Want to Do with My Life?

years lisotening to other people tell me what my vision should be and what I should be doing. It is very liberating, but also a lot of hard work, to say, "This is what I want to do."

So here is the vision that I have prepared for you: "I, Paisly, will dedicate my life to making my Grandpa successful and happy." This is the sort of vision that others will impose on you. It does not take into account that you have a mind of your own or that you might have dreams of your own, too.

In addition, when you say "this is what I want to do," you need to realize that when you get up each morning, the world will be a different place than it was when you went to bed the night before. Change is constant, so keep your eyes open for new opportunities that others may not have noticed.

You also need to consider what you want from a marriage. If you want a husband who remains a teenager at heart all his life, and expects his wife to not only keep a beautiful, well-run house, but also to go out and earn the money, so he can spend his time hunting, fishing, golfing, or pursuing some other hobby, then all you have to do is grab the first young man who proposes to you. If you want something else in life, then you need to be more selective. At some point in the future, you may even have to tell yourself that even though you love a young man, he won't help you reach your goals. Don't start squawking. You want a husband who is a partner. Taking the time to find the right one will make your life more rewarding.

Grandpa, Help!

Now, all that's left is finding a mountaintop on the beach at Waikiki so you can build your castle. Remember, at this point we're not talking about developing a vision that is fully practical. Come up with wild ideas. Decide what your dreams are. Then get your vision down on paper or saved on your computer. Decide where you want to be in five years, in ten years, and in twenty years.

Later we will look at the vision. Actually, you will look at the vision, and I hope you will invite me to look at it with you. However, you must remain in control of the vision. It is your vision, not mine. This second look is when you can begin to decide what is practical. You might decide that rather than building a mountain for your castle on the beach at Waikiki, it would be better to move inland a couple of miles where mountains already exist.

After your vision has been refined, you can start determining what you will need to do in order to reach it. To have a successful buggy whip company, you're going to need to figure out a way to eliminate the internal combustion engine. Then you need to decide how to make our roads, streets, highways, and inter-state highway systems horse-drawn-carriage friendly. Once you determine what needs to be done, set practical goals. After the goals are set, you should select a way to monitor your progress.

I suspect at this point you're giggling again. This whole process, while it is serious, should be a tremendous amount of fun. Take the time, and keep coming

What Do I Want to Do with My Life?

back to it. Even after you have finished everything, keep working at it, because setting a vision and developing goals is kind of like driving a car. As you're driving down the highway, occasionally you have to make corrections with the steering wheel; otherwise, you might cross the center line and run into another vehicle or end up in a ditch. Those are not the outcomes you want.

I love you,
and I want to see you reach your goals,
no matter how impractical I think they are,
Grandpa

Dearest Grandpa,

You can make me laugh without even trying. Maybe you should have been a talk show host on late night TV.

It is your very practical advice and your willingness to open up and admit what you think are your failings that make me open up and come to you for guidance. Besides, you are never judgmental, no matter what I do. You say, "My father once told me ..." or "My mother told me a story about ...." Then you tell a story about some animal, and woven into the story will be the life lesson that I needed. You know, you should do more marketing for *Animals I Have Hated*, and you should finish up *Another Book of Stories*. There are people who need those books. If I were to focus on helping you for a few months, I would be

Grandpa, Help!

helping others, too. See, you are helping me set my vision and reach my goals.

> *By the way, I love you more.*
> *Your favorite granddaughter,*
> *Paisly*

Grandpa's Note: *You notice that Paisly and I often end with an "I love you more" comment. This is a game we play, and I have been known to say, "I love you a quarter of an inch more than you love me." Can you tell me what that means? We have no idea what it means, but we enjoy using it. We never say, "I would love you more if you did...." That would be trying to control the other one and that is unhealthy.*

This chapter will be the lead chapter in the book Grandpa Help!— Dreams, Visions, Passions, & Goals. Check NordyBooks.com and Grandpa-Help.com for the publication date.

This is the final chapter of this volume. The pages that follow contain information about the authors, a list of our other books, and a brief epilogue.

What Do I Want to Do with My Life?

A Little About Grandpa

Much of my early education came from the animal stories my mother told. There was a life lesson woven into each of her stories. Much of my later education came from animals I observed. These stories can be found in *Animals I Have Hated*. When I was eleven years old, my father decided he needed an education in chemistry. Since my mother was a chemist, we sat down at the kitchen table three nights per week and studied first chemistry and later cement chemistry. After all of this, the high school I attended insisted that I take a chemistry class. Can you imagine how much of a brat I was in that class? The teacher admitted before the year was over that I knew more chemistry than he did, and he did not renew his contract for the following year. Before I was eighteen, I was Assistant to the Head of Research and Development for Pozzolana, Inc., and Rio Clay Products.

Since I could not wait to get a real education and a real job, I enrolled in college. With a little time out for military service and my Grand Tour in Southeast Asia,

I ended up with a graduate degree in aquatic ecology, with an emphasis on aquatic chemistry. After working in that field for a few years, I got back to doing what I learned at our kitchen table.

The only degree I ever displayed on my office wall was my eighth-grade diploma. The other formal education did not apply. When I was Head of Research and Development, new employees were often taken to my office so they could look at that diploma, signed by Mr. Harmon L. McClellan. Then they were told, "See what he has done. If you apply yourself, there is no reason why you cannot rise as high in this company as he has risen."

I have been married twice. The first one ended in divorce. It was all her fault. About four years later, though, I grew up enough to realize that we were both still kids when we got married, even though we had been in our mid-twenties. We were also both at fault.

Since my second marriage occurred after I realized that I was partially at fault for the first marriage breaking up, it has been much more successful. It has lasted more than thirty years.

Many have claimed that I am a world-class expert in several areas. One becomes an expert by gaining experience. One gains experience by making blunders. I guess if you compare the number of blunders I have made with the number of blunders others have made, I must be a world-class expert. By sharing my experience, I hope to keep you from making the same blunders that I made.

A Little About Grandpa

A Little About Haleigh

Haleigh is sixteen. She has long, dark hair and the body of an athlete in training. That's because she is an athlete in training. She is a long-distance runner, a dancer, and a kayaker. Besides that, she studies the violin and creative writing. When I'm teaching kayaking classes, she often serves as my assistant. She attends a high school for the arts.

Haleigh tends to be blunt and concrete in her thinking. She leads by charging forward with good ideas. One day we had a kayaking group out running Class I rapids. We stopped for a break, and Haleigh asked where we were going next. Jokingly, I told her we were going to go back to the launch site. She took the statement seriously, hopped in her kayak, and paddled upstream. She made it through several strong Class I rapids before she turned over and we managed to catch up with her. We were following the footpath along the river. If we had been in our kayaks, we would not have been able to catch her. Can you imagine what she said to me when I told her that I had been joking? She said more than that.

Grandpa, Help!

In October 2012, Haleigh developed a stress fracture in her leg, sucked up the pain, and ran in two cross-country meets. She did horribly, in her estimation. For her worst race, she came in 35th out of over 200 participants. She did that with a broken *fibula*. I sure would not want to meet her in a dark alley when she was mad at me.

In November, with her broken leg, she helped me take fourteen military officers on a kayaking trip. When some of them did not follow instructions and ended up in a pileup en masse in a rapid, she participated fully in the swift water rescues. She stayed in her kayak and worked from below, going in and pulling people out and later pulling kayaks out. Then she called the group together and dressed them down like a First Sergeant. They took the dressing-down.

She plans on attending medical school and becoming a dermatologist.

A Little About Haleigh

A Little About Paisly

Paisly is about two months younger than Haleigh and has the thickest head of hair that I can ever recall encountering. Recently, after going through a full-body scan at the airport, Paisly spent what seemed like ten minutes letting an agent check her hair to determine what type of weapon she was carrying. The agent commented that no one has that much hair.

Paisly loves photography and is good at it.

Paisly also loves people and has hundreds of friends. She dislikes confronting people; as a result, she would never take on the First Sergeant role that Haleigh took on. Paisly leads by developing a consensus among her peers. As a result, many of her friends do not realize that they are being led.

In her junior year in high school, Paisly was elected president of her class. Rather than campaign, she got her friends to make posters, put them up, and then recruit their friends to do the same. Her campaign slogan was "Pick Paisly, not your nose." If I had told Paisly that we were going to paddle upstream through rapids, she would have laughed and asked me when I was going to get started.

Since then Paisly has dropped out of school and is pursuing her education on-line. Much of what I write, Paisly gets the first look at and tends to keep the writing focus on our topic. I like to wander around.

You see Paisly at her best when you read the chapter *I'm Going to Give You a Kiss.*

A Little About Paisly

Bonding w/ Granddaughters

In April 2011, I took a group on a kayak-camping trip on the Rio Bravo del Norte, so we could study Native American art in the caves. The trip involved one night of camping with our vehicles parked close to the campsite and two nights of camping in caves above the river. We fought the wind most of the time that we paddled. We were paddling into whitecaps part of the time, which meant that the wind was over 21 miles per hour. It was a trip that challenged the stamina of all of us. During the trip, we also celebrated Paisly's Quinceañera in a cave. A quinceañera is a fifteenth birthday party for a young lady and usually involves an elaborate party and a formal dance. We bonded on that trip as we had never bonded before.

That trip resulted in several devotions, one of which follows. This devotion illustrates how differently the two young ladies reacted to my attempt to protect my new sleeping bags and air mattresses.

Grandpa, Help!

Washing Feet

John 13:12-17 When he had washed their feet and put on his outer garments and resumed his place, he said to them, "Do you understand what I have done to you? You call me Teacher and Lord, and you are right, for so I am. If I then, your Lord and Teacher, have washed your feet, you also ought to wash one another's feet. For I have given you an example, that you also should do just as I have done to you. Truly, truly, I say to you, a servant is not greater than his master, nor is a messenger greater than the one who sent him. If you know these things, blessed are you if you do them." (ESV)

We were camping in a cave, and it came time to bed down. I noticed my granddaughters' feet were filthy. They would be sleeping on new air mattresses and in new sleeping bags. To protect my investment, I proceeded to wash their feet. Paisly said that it reminded her of Jesus washing His disciples' feet. The comment made me feel warm inside. I was performing a very humble act for a selfish reason, yet she made it seem like a wonderful act of service. I was being praised by a special young lady. Then my granddaughter Haleigh said that all men are evil, and therefore they could not remind her of Jesus. I'm sure she was using the words "all men" to refer to

Bonding w/ Granddaughters

all humans rather than just to me and other males of the species. She had a point. We are all sinful, but she allowed me to wash her feet. I resisted the very strong temptation to tickle them. After their feet were washed, they went to bed. Within a few minutes I was in bed and sound asleep.

This reminds me that Christ came to earth to serve and save us. We serve our Lord and Savior Jesus Christ by serving others. Many of these acts of service are very humble acts. A friend of mine washed dishes at potluck meals, saying that she was washing dishes for the Lord.

Lord, help me to find humble acts of service to bring glory to Your Name. Amen.

After the trip was over, one of the other participants told me that each night after I was sound asleep, my two granddaughters were up running around getting their feet dirty again. That explained the crusted mud in the bottom of the sleeping bags. I had to grin and remember what my old friend Bobby Burns said in his poem, *To a Mouse*, "The best laid plans of mice and men oft times go asunder." But I did end up with some great granddaughters out of it.

Grandpa, Help!

Who Are Abuelo and Nieta?

Mi Abuelo,

OH! I was watching a commercial on TV the other day, and there was an older lady who the children called Abuelita. After wondering why that sounded so familiar, I realized it meant "little grandmother" in Spanish. "Abuelita" sounds familiar because ever since you took me to the Alamo and showed me how well-meaning people caused problems by using the wrong materials to repair it, I have called you "Abuelo."

Te amo (an endearing form of "I love you"),
Nieta

Nieta,

When we visited the Alamo, you signed us in as Paisly y Abuelo. That is Paisly and Grandfather. Having a pet name for a loved one is a way of making that loved one feel special. I could always call you Paisly, but calling you Nieta, which is Spanish for "granddaughter," is a special name that you and I

Grandpa, Help!

understand. Since we had just celebrated your Quinceañera (a lady's fifteenth birthday celebration) the week before while camped in a cave on the Rio Bravo del Norte, it seemed appropriate to use Spanish.

We had fun poking around the Alamo looking at how masonry cement plaster was used in an attempt to repair walls of limestone block bedded in adobe mortar. The modern craftsmen did not understand how different the materials were. You seemed thrilled to listen to me. It made my day. Later, after reading what you wrote on your father's website about our inspection of the Alamo and the other Spanish missions in San Antonio, I knew that not only did you enjoy yourself, but you also retained much of what I told you.

At one of the Spanish missions, you saw a Jr. Ranger Badge that a child could earn. You asked for the paperwork, and the Ranger thought it was a little strange since the program was aimed at elementary school students. You asked if there was an age limit. There was not, so you earned your Jr. Ranger Badge and wore it proudly. I'm surprised that you did not get me involved in earning my own Jr. Ranger Badge.

It is so delightful that you can go from being a rational adult one minute to being a little girl the next. As you go through life, please keep that ability. If you become a writer, and I think you will end up writing a great deal, that dual perspective will greatly enhance your writing ability.

Te amo mucho,
Abuelo

Who Are Abuelo and Nieta?

Books

Recommended Reading

Success Before Sex
  by Sharnice A. Jones
  After you read this book, you will understand
  why it is the first book on the recommended
  reading list. Every teenager, parent, and grandparent should read it. The author wrote this book
  when she was 17 years old. It is better-researched
  and more-readable than many books written by
  authors with letters behind their names. Ms.
  Jones speaks from the heart and powerfully de-
  livers the message that if a young lady gets
  pregnant before she has an education and has
  started on the pathway to success, she will be
  limiting her own future as well as that of her
  child.

Grandpa, Help!

Boundaries with Kids - How Healthy Choices Grow Healthy Children
> by Dr. Henry Cloud & Dr. John Townsend
> This book is written for parents; but by both the teen and the parents reading it, it will help develop a better understanding of each culture.

Boundaries with Teens: When to Say Yes, How to Say No
> by John Townsend
> This book is written for parents; but by both the teen and the parents reading it, it will help develop a better understanding of each culture.

How to Find Your Soulmate Without Losing Your Soul
> by Jason and Crystalina Evert
> In your quest for love, don't lose yourself along the way. While navigating through the dating scene, every woman begins to wonder: How do I know when a guy really loves me? Am I being too picky? Do I even deserve love? Is my relationship worth keeping? Is love worth the risk? Are any decent guys left? This book helps you navigate through these perilous waters.

Recommended Reading

POLISHED My Financial Manicure
     by Brandi Minter
     Do you enjoy getting pampered at the beauty or
     nail salon? Your financial health is more impor-
     tant than your hair or nails. This book helps
     pamper you as you improve your financial
     health.

*Rich Habits - The Daily Success Habits of
Wealthy Individuals*
     by Thomas C. Corley
     People who are successful usually have habits
     that are substantially different from the habits of
     those who are not successful. Often the assump-
     tion is made that successful people have better
     luck than those who are not as successful. That is
     true, but successful people create most of their
     luck with their habits. If you want to be ordinary,
     fine, but if you have serious goals you want to ac-
     complish, you need this book.

*Smart Money Smart Kids: Raising the Next
Generation to Win with Money*
     by Dave Ramsey & Rachel Cruze
     This book is aimed at parents who want to teach
     their children how to win with money, but con-
     sider reading it with your grandchildren and then
     discussing the issues. The book starts with the
     basics like working, spending, saving, and giving.
     It then explores more challenging issues like

avoiding debt for life, paying for college with cash, and battling discontentment.

The Holy Bible
Especially the book of Proverbs
Proverbs 31:10 - 31 offers some wisdom on the qualities of a wife.
The Song of Solomon describes love within a marriage.

Recommended Reading

Books by the Nordmeyers

Published Books

You can find out more about our books by going to www.NordyBooks.com/.

The Stucco Book - The Basics - Everything you need to know to complete a perfect conventional stucco job.

by Herb Nordmeyer Everything you need to know to complete a conventional stucco job, whether you are a Do-It-Yourselfer or a seasoned professional. This easy-to-read book is packed with information you can use. Available where good books are sold on-line.

Animals I Have Hated - Howl-arious Life Lessons Taught by Animals

by Herb Nordmeyer
A collection of true animal stories that are also life lessons. The author learned some of these stories from his mother as he was growing up, and he experienced others firsthand. If you are a grandparent, this book will probably bring back memories. You will also want to share it with your grandchildren, since it is a fun way to learn some of the lessons we all need. Available where good books are sold on-line.

We Heard the Wings of Angels

A collection of 32 devotions written by and for cancer patients and their families. Available free of charge by downloading a PDF copy from the NordyBooks.com website.

Books by the Nordmeyers

Cancer—An Intense House Guest
A booklet of practical advice for living with cancer, such as having your teeth cleaned before starting Chemo if you want to have your teeth after you finish. Available free of charge by downloading a PDF copy from the NordyBooks website.

Living with Cancer - That Intense Houseguest

by Judy & Herb Nordmeyer
Cancer barged in and set up housekeeping. In this book, we provide practical advice for people with cancer, their families, and their friends. It is not meant as a spiritual guide; however, we cannot separate our spiritual lives from the rest of our experience. We want to help you develop answers that work for you as you evict the Intense Houseguest. You can get it for $0.99 from Kindle, but it is available free of charge at Smashwords.com. Easiest way to find it is to search for "Nordmeyer" on the Smashwords.com website.

Grandpa Help!

Grandpa, Help! Answer to Questions a Young Lady Would Never Ash Her Parents

by Herb Nordmeyer and his granddaughters Kindle ebook edition was published in April 2013, and just over a year later we are publishing the print edition. This is a serious advice book written in an easy to understand format and is seasoned with a great deal of humor. Young ladies have commented that this is the book they need. Middle-aged ladies comment they wish they had this book when they were dating. Grandmothers comment that it brings back so many memories of the mistakes they made as teenagers. This is the first book in the *Grandpa, Help!* series.

Books by the Nordmeyers

Coming Soon

Grandpa, Help! - Dating - Is it Love or Lust
>by Herb Nordmeyer and his granddaughters
It will be published initially as a Kindle ebook, and then we will follow within a few months with a print book. Editing is complete, and we are working on a cover. We anticipate publishing in July, 2014.

Grandpa Helps Grandparents
>by Herb Nordmeyer and Sylvia Scheid
Since numerous young ladies have adopted Herb Nordmeyer as their grandpa, at the writing workshop in Dallas, TX, in December, 2012, Grandpa and Sylvia were strongly encouraged to write a book to help grandparents connect to their grandchildren. The book is in the final editing process. We anticipate publishing in July, 2014, as an ebook and as a print book.

The Stucco Book - Forensics & Repairs
>by Herb Nordmeyer
When shortcuts are taken, stucco can fail. Before a repair can be effectively made, the cause of the failure needs to be identified and corrected. This book contains a lifetime of determining causes and figuring out how to effectively repair the problem. We are aiming for publication in December, 2014.

Grandpa, Help!

The Adhered Concrete Masonry Veneer Book
by Rick Garagliano and Herb Nordmeyer
Adhered Concrete Masonry Veneer is a growing
industry, but mistakes which lead to problems
are being made in installations. This is the first
comprehensive book on the subject. It is also fas-
cinating to read, since both Rick and Herb bring
their unique brands of humor and easy writing
styles to the book. We are aiming for publication
in December, 2014.

Books by the Nordmeyers

Epilogue

This is the advice Herb gives to his granddaughters. Some may disagree with him, but keep in mind a quote Herb learned when he was in school back when the dinosaurs were still roaming the earth. William Ernest Henley ended his poem, "Invictus," with the words, "I am the master of my fate. I am the captain of my soul."

Grandpa's Note*: The dinosaur statement comes from an 8th grader in a Sunday School class I was teaching some years ago who very seriously asked me if I was sad when the dinosaurs died.*

The decisions you make will impact your future. Decide what you want your future to be, and then make appropriate decisions. If you are planning on becoming a doctor, can you afford a teenage pregnancy?

If you cannot afford a teenage pregnancy, can you afford to have sex, since no form of birth control works all of the time?

Grandpa, Help!

If you cannot afford to have sex, can you afford to make out with your boyfriend with some or all of your clothes off?

The urges you have and the boys you associate with are no different than the urges that people have had for as long as there have been people. Many of the consequences are different. Many a young lady a few thousand years ago was stoned to death for letting a boy have his way. In most cultures, we have gotten away from that practice. When I was young, I commonly heard, "The first baby can come at any time. The rest take nine months." Some of the girls, when I was going to school, suddenly moved off to stay with their relatives. Back alley abortions, followed by death-causing infections, were common.

The pill and abortion on demand in sanitary conditions reduced, but did not eliminate, the risk of having a baby out of wedlock. Political correctness removed "bastard" from the language to describe the baby born out of wedlock.

Things are not better than they used to be, they are different. If you have a child before you have completed your education, and especially if you are not married to the father, you are probably going to live in poverty and your children will spend their lives in poverty. Is that the goal you have for them? If you get a sanitary and legal abortion, will you wake up in the middle of the night haunted by that action?

In all aspects of your life, determine where you want to be and then determine the values and goals

Epilogue

you need to get there. While making the appropriate decisions will not guarantee that you will get where you want to go, making the wrong decisions will certainly guarantee that you will not get to where you want to go.

Herb's granddaughters know that he loves them without reservation. No matter what they do, he will still love them. He even continues to love the one who did the unmentionable thing of getting a tattoo. The bond is so strong that the young lady knew that her grandpa would continue to love her even though he disliked tattoos. Many of you reading this series of books do not have the advantage of unconditional love. That makes your journey harder.

We are writing this series of books to help make your journey a little easier. Paisly will be developing a forum on our website, www.GrandpaHelp.com, where you can ask questions and discuss things. You may address your questions and comments to Paisly, to Herb, or to the forum at large. If you address them to Herb, you may refer to him as Herb or as Mr. Nordmeyer, or you can make his day and refer to him as Grandpa. Paisly and Haleigh have learned that by calling him Grandpa, they can wrap him around their little fingers.

If you do not have a grandparent you can talk to, find one and do what Paisly and Haleigh did. Adopt one. If your newly adopted grandparent, or your biological grandparent, needs help, we are working on a book to help grandparents bond with grandchildren.

Grandpa, Help!

Aim for the stars, or wherever you want to go in life, and make decisions appropriate for reaching your goals, not our goals, not your parents' goals, and not your teachers' goals. When you stumble, dust yourself off and continue. We wish you success and happiness in life.

Paisly   Grandpa   Haleigh

Epilogue

CPSIA information can be obtained
at www.ICGtesting.com
Printed in the USA
FFOW05n1256100714

9 780996 010009